The Occult Explosion

**An Examination of Psychic Mysteries and
Modern Witchcraft**

An enlarged revision of
the author's *Secrets of the Spirit World*

Roy Allan Anderson, D.D., F.R.G.S. (London)

Pacific Press Publishing Association
Mountain View, California
Oshawa, Ontario

Cover photo by D. Tank

ISBN 0-8163-0548-X

Contents

Introduction

Imagine my surprise, and the astonishment of millions, when we awakened on April 25, 1982, to read in our morning papers a full-page ad proclaiming, "THE CHRIST IS NOW HERE."

I learned later that this same ad appeared in about twenty major cities around the world. The ad went on to say: "How will we recognize him? Look for a modern man concerned with modern problems—political, economic, and social. Since July, 1977, the Christ has been emerging as a spokesman for a group or community in a well-known modern country. He is not a religious leader, but an educator in the broadest sense of the word—pointing the way out of our present crisis. We will recognize Him by His extraordinary spiritual potency, the universality of His viewpoint, and His love for all humanity. He comes not to judge but to aid and inspire."

Biblical students recognize a problem here because Christ Himself, in Matthew 24, has told the world how He will return and what counterfeit deceptions the world could expect prior to His coming.

The point I am making in this book is that we live in a generation when the appeal to the occult, to the supernatural, has never been more universal and sophisticated. No longer is the occult only a matter of dark rooms, burning candles, and moving tables. Networks of prominent organizations feature world leaders who are, in varying degrees of awareness, promoting a New World Order that will preempt Christianity while endorsing positions espoused by those sponsoring this astonishing newspaper ad.

When Hitler took control of Germany, occultism in that country was widespread. Billy Graham observed that "interest in the occult in any nation grows in direct proportion to the depth of the spiritual vacuum in that country." He further pointed out that "there is a connection between the increase of drugs, pornography, sexual license, and the occult in the U.S."

Many are making the comparison between the 1920s and the 1980s. They see not only the economic similarities with its twin consequences of unemployment and stagnation/inflation but also the bewilderment of so many as they search for meaning and hope. The occult explosion of the last fifteen years especially is no accident or coincidence. It is humanity's search for assurance as it reaches out beyond itself for answers to earth's biggest problems.

Most surprising is the rise of the occult in Communist countries. Until a few years ago, they had no place for the supernatural in their materialistic philosophy. For generations not one parapsychologist could be found in the U.S.S.R. But today top-level Soviet physiologists, biologists, geologists, and others are steeped in ESP research. Bulgaria boasts of more psychics than perhaps any other country in Europe.

This amazing worldwide interest in the occult is not a passing fad. We can expect even more astounding claims and events in the immediate future. How should thinking people respond to these claims? How should they relate to physical phenomena that defy normal tests of reality?

For example, how should thinking people relate to Dr. Norman Vincent Peale's recent interview in a magazine read by millions, where he recounts his experiences with his dead relatives, encounters that prove to him that there is life after death and that we can communicate with the dead.

This book emphasizes the biblical position on the spirit world. More than that, it shows how Christians in all ages have found wisdom and strength from the Lord in dealing with occult phenomena. Paul said, "Be strong in the Lord, and in the power of his might." Ephesians 6:10.

We urge that the reader reserve judgment if still in doubt until the amazing story of the occult explosion has been more fully presented in this book.

Roy Allan Anderson, D.D., F.R.G.S.

Behind Closed Doors

"I'm through with God!" he shouted as I stepped into his office. "I don't want you here. In fact, I don't want to see you again—ever! I'm through!"

Strange words from a friend, especially when we had been so close. I had always been welcomed into his office, but not that morning. What had gone wrong? What had changed his attitude?

I soon discovered the reason. He had just returned from a spiritualistic séance, the first he had attended for many years. To him it was unfortunate that I arrived just at that moment. He was still revelling in the aftereffects of his conversation with an important apparition, a "Pharaoh" of ancient Egypt. The atmosphere was tense. This was a showdown, and we both knew it!

The first time I met this city official and his family was at a large evangelistic meeting. I was in New Zealand at that time, and at that meeting I had spoken on "The Bible as the Word of God." This man and his wife and three daughters made themselves known to me, and invited me to visit them at their hilltop home. I was happy to go. They were very friendly, and before long they looked upon me as "one of the family."

Not only the father and the mother, but also the three girls, studied the Bible eagerly with me. From the very first, however, I noticed something unusual about that father; he never seemed completely at ease when we touched the question of death and the resurrection. Later I learned that he had been a member of an important spiritualistic circle and for years had practiced clairvoyance, even serving as a medium. But that was twenty-five years

7

before. Since then he had never attended a spiritualistic meeting or a séance.

He was an important figure in that city. He had never been a Christian; and when I met him, he seemed to be entirely irreligious. When I got closer to him, I learned he had a constant companion—a "familiar spirit," as the Bible terms it. Leviticus 19:31. It claimed to be a female spirit, and while not visible to anyone else, yet that power was there continually, I later learned. She called herself "Nancy," and was as real to him as any member of his family. She was tall, with long, flowing tresses.

He rarely made a decision without consulting that spirit, and remarkably, he got his answers. If he needed a direct Yes or No, he would quietly appeal to this spirit entity and his hand would be lifted six or eight inches from the desk and the number of thumps would indicate the decision. When once that power took control, neither he nor anyone else could hold that arm still. He was no weakling; on the contrary, he stood about six feet four in height. He was well-built, and weighed 225 pounds. In his younger days he had been a champion heavyweight boxer. Apart from those rather simple responses from "Nancy," spiritualism apparently played no part in his life.

"Familiar Spirit" Turns Enemy

During those twenty-five years he encountered no problem with the spirits, but when once he began to study the Bible, things changed rapidly. Of course, he was well acquainted with unseen powers; but he came to know that such powers are not all from God. Some are definitely evil. Learning what the Bible says on this subject, he decided to have nothing more to do with spirits.

Once having made his decision, he began to encounter real opposition. The first came from the spirit "Nancy." When she failed to turn him against the Bible, a whole group of spirits united to withstand him. Still he and his family continued to study the Word of God. Sometimes we studied together late into the night.

Before long the spirits began to oppose me personally, first by argument, then by physical force. One night as we finished our study of the twelfth chapter of Revelation, the spirits said to him: "What you have been discussing here tonight is all wrong. We have the key to the whole situation, and we give you this as the symbol.'' With those words a large key, nearly eight inches long, fell to the floor from apparently nowhere. All were startled. Then one of the girls reached over and picked it up. No one had ever seen it before.

On another occasion, an apparition appeared in the form of the family's pet dog, a champion fox terrier, which had recently died. For years the husband and father had bred champions. And when that sharp-nosed little creature jumped up on his lap in the accustomed way, the family was, of course, deeply impressed. But by that time they all knew something of the deceptive power of the spirit world. What seemed almost overwhelming evidence of survival after death, they knew was just another effort by evil spirits to deceive. Apparitions in the form of animals are not uncommon.

Unseen Hands Clutch My Throat

Many strange things happened during the next few months, for the battle was growing more intense. Sometimes as I left that home the spirits would say: ''We will get rid of Anderson tonight on his way home.'' And they often tried! More than once I have felt the stranglehold of unseen hands clutching my throat and forcing me to the ground. There is no question in one's mind concerning the existence of invisible powers when he is faced with such experiences as these.

I knew I was wrestling ''not against flesh and blood,'' as the apostle Paul said, but ''against wicked spirits in high places.'' Ephesians 6:12, margin. How wicked these spirits really are I came to realize when, for example, that father, moved by one of these evil intelligences, grasped his seventeen-year-old daughter by the throat and with fingers that seemed like steel began choking her to death. Under normal circumstances he was the embodiment of kindness. But on this occasion he flew into a towering rage because she had declared that the Bible was indeed the Word of God and the only safe guide. Sensing her danger, I stepped forward and in the name of the Lord Jesus Christ commanded him to release her. His grip relaxed immediately.

For months I studied the Bible with that New Zealand family. In fact, I lived with the family for three months while my wife and little son were visiting loved ones in Australia. It gave me an eerie feeling to hear, as I did many times, that father pass my door in the middle of the night and go down the stairway to the living room. I knew why he was going. It was to hold a private séance. And when he got there, the piano would usually start playing of its own accord. He was no musician; he did not know one note from another, but the piano played by itself. It was always the same song, about Polly who died and was now looking down from heaven.

The months I spent as a guest in that home were pleasurable in most ways, but also a real strain. To battle with evil powers for the soul of a man, and sense the struggle becoming more intense with every passing week, is something one would not willingly choose. We worshiped together each day, and it was a joy to see those dear folk taking hold of God's Word.

After my wife and little son returned from Australia and we were back in our own home again, I was awakened one morning about five o'clock by a voice which spoke as clearly and distinctly as any I have ever heard. The words were those of our Lord Himself: "This kind goeth not out but by prayer and fasting."

At once I recognized this as a call from God. I awakened my wife, and we prayed earnestly. We both were convinced that God wanted me to visit this man in his office. His work in that city was akin to that of a magistrate and was particularly concerned with pensions. He was a well-respected citizen, and his office was in the heart of the business section.

Before going to see him, I stopped at the office of a doctor friend, in whose prayers I had occasion to have real confidence. We had prayed through many situations before. So, while his patients waited, I related to him the happenings of that morning. Together we sought God's help for whatever lay ahead.

The "White Wings of Egypt"

When I arrived at this man's office, so familiar to me, he blurted out: "Anderson, what are you doing here? I don't want to see you again—ever!" He had a look of hatred in his eyes. As already mentioned, he was a massively built man, and as a police officer and a detective he had been trained to brook no argument from anyone. Now he was demon-possessed, and he really looked it!

"I'm through with God," he shouted.

"But God is not through with you," I replied.

"Why should I bother with God? I have the highest honor that can ever come to a man," he said.

"What is that?" I asked.

"I have the 'White Wings of Egypt,' " he said sneeringly. "And no harm can ever come to me. The spirits have assured me that I can go anywhere, and my life is perfectly safe."

Then with a fiendish chuckle he told how he had gone to a spirit medium early that morning. He related how he had commanded the medium to bring up for him one of the ancient "Pharaohs," calling him by name. The medium became alarmed and begged to be excused, for she said: "You evidently belong to a higher circle of spirits from those I know, and the one you are calling is very high. Please, don't use me—go to someone else."

For the moment he became the old police officer, and demanded obedience. She was soon in a trance. When the "Pharaoh" apparition appeared, he claimed to have a special message for him. "You must stop studying the Bible," the "Pharaoh" ordered. "I have greater truth than that old obsolete book."

During that séance this man also communed with another spirit purporting to be his first wife, who had died more than twenty years earlier. To prove her identity this apparition rubbed a handkerchief across his hands, laden with perfume—the same perfume he had given his bride on the night of their wedding. And I can testify that when I met him a few minutes later his hands exuded perfume in such quantity that the office was filled with the odor. Of course some doubter will say he had the perfume in his office all the time. But none who have had experience with unseen powers will find cause for doubt.

When that spirit interview came to a close, the "Pharaoh" conferred on him the covering of the "White Wings of Egypt," saying, "This is a special honor. The highest honor we can ever give to a human being and it comes to you with the blessing of all ancient Egypt."

When that man came back to his office, he was elated. His whole countenance was changed. Just then I arrived and walked straight in, as usual.

But things were not as usual. He was belligerent and wanted nothing to do with me or with God. Here was a desperate situation and it presented a real challenge. There sat my friend, the one in whose home I had spent months in happy fellowship as we studied the Word of God together. Now he was far from God, blaspheming His name, and defiantly ordering me out of his office. Repeatedly he shouted: "I'm through with God."

What could I do? Should I leave as he had ordered me, or should I defy the spirits? I moved closer to him and, putting my hand on his shoulder, took an old Bible from the shelf in his office. It was the one he used when individuals were required to give information under oath.

An Astounding Answer

I moved slowly, for I was lifting my heart silently to God in prayer. I fingered the pages for a moment, and then in a strange way that Bible seemed to open naturally at the thirtieth chapter of Isaiah. I began to read aloud: "Woe to the rebellious children, said the Lord, that take counsel, but not of Me; and that cover with a covering, but not of My Spirit, that they may add sin to sin: that walk to go down into Egypt, and have not asked at My mouth; to strengthen themselves in the strength of Pharaoh, and to trust in the shadow of Egypt! Therefore shall the strength of Pharaoh be your shame, and the trust in the shadow of Egypt your confusion." Isaiah 30:1-3.

He jumped up, grabbed the Bible out of my hand, and shouted: "That's not there—you're making it up!"

"It *is* there," I replied. "Read it yourself."

He took the Bible in his trembling hands and reread those verses aloud. Then he slumped back into his chair as if he had been struck.

Kindly but firmly I said, "Dad,"—for that's what I called him—"the road you have taken is the road to confusion and ultimate destruction, and you know it. You are putting your trust in the 'shadow of Egypt.' You are boasting of a covering, the 'White Wings of Egypt.' You know this is not of God's Spirit; it is the spirit of the devil. In doing this you are adding sin to sin."

He was silent. While he looked wistfully into my face, I read these words in the next chapter. "Woe to them that go down to Egypt for help; . . . but they look not unto the Holy One of Israel, neither seek the Lord!" Isaiah 31:1.

He looked very solemn as he sat there. Then he stepped from his desk and walked over to the door, locking it so that we would not be interrupted. Looking into my eyes, he said: "What shall I do?"

I said: "Let us pray to God for forgiveness and deliverance."

He joined me in prayer. We offered up earnest petitions that day in his office, and I saw that man claim the victory. It was marvelous to witness his turning from darkness to light. But I had a feeling that the great deceiver would not give up the fight without a struggle. During the next few days some of us who were close friends of this man fasted and prayed that full deliverance might come to him.

Some weeks later, following a wonderful day of worship, I felt impressed to go and see this man, for he had absented himself from church that day. I took a friend with me, a courageous man who had been decorated for gallantry as an airman in World War I. Before going up to the house we prayed, and then I phoned to say we were coming. The wife met us at the door and led us into the living room. As soon as I entered, I sensed that things were anything but reassuring, for there sat our friend in silent communion with the spirits. I had seen him on other occasions sitting on the davenport talking to his spirit friend, "Nancy." He spoke no words. It was thought communion.

Spirits' Last Desperate Attempt

We waited a few minutes; then, beginning our conversation in a casual strain at first, I tried to open up the question we wanted to discuss with him. That very day the church had decided to ask his wife to serve as a deaconess. As soon as I mentioned that, his attitude changed. He became adamant, and for an hour and a half he opposed everything we suggested. Seeing we were getting nowhere, I rose to leave. In doing so, however, I said: "I have never left this home without having prayer, and I do not intend to tonight. Let us kneel together."

This took him somewhat off guard. Naturally he was in no

mood to pray, but out of respect he cooperated. He had the same leering smirk that I had seen at other times when he had been communing with spirits. In our family worships this man always knelt at a certain place in that room, using the piano stool for support. I suggested that he do so again. He did, but reluctantly.

Then I asked the friend I had brought to pray. Scarcely had he begun when I sensed something was wrong. My friend seemed hardly able to speak. I knew what it was, for I, myself, was passing through the same experience. We were being "pressured" by an unseen power. It is a harrowing experience to feel every inch of one's body under pressure, which becomes stronger every moment. We could scarcely breathe, much less speak.

Then the door opened of its own accord and in came a huge apparition, appearing as a knight in shining armor and holding aloft an upturned Turkish scimitar. At the sight, my friend, this powerfully built former police officer and leader of a detective squad, sprang from his place. Throwing one arm around his wife's neck and the other around mine, he clung to us, trembling like a frightened child!

The situation was desperate, for this spirit threatened to kill him. Summoning all the strength I could, I challenged, "In the name of Jesus Christ, I command the devils to leave this house at once."

What followed was terrific! Never before or since have I heard anything like it. All hell seemed to break loose! Windows rattled, doors slammed, and the whole house shook as if by an earthquake. We heard shrieking and yelling. The house rocked, but we remained on our knees until at last the uproar ceased. The calm that followed was as impressive as the tumult before.

As we rose from our knees, we looked at each other in amazement. That man's look of terror was gone, but he was still shaking. Now he knew that God was there, in the very place which had been rattled by the powers of hell. He also knew that the power of Jesus Christ is far greater than that of Satan.

To call upon the name of Jesus for protection and then feel the viselike grip of the enemy relax is tremendous. More than a year passed, however, before my friend was really free. I know that spiritualists will say that those opposing powers were "bad spirits,'' but that the "good spirits" can be trusted, for they protect and never harm. That is exactly what this man himself believed when first we met. For remember: he, too, had been a leading spiritualist. But he soon discovered, as thousands of others have, that even the so-called "good spirits" of the occult are deceivers. They will use their powers against the very ones who once paid them homage.

What are we to make of all of this? Are these things just the product of excited minds? Or mere fancy? Who are these beings which at times appear? This is our quest in the following chapters.

The Spirit Powers of the Adversary

A large meeting was being held at the popular Foresters Hall in the heart of London's West End. A fellow minister and friend of mine, Elman Folkenberg, was making his way to that lecture and happened to meet a couple who were bound for the same place. The couple said they had never attended anything of the kind before and were a little skeptical about the fantastic claims the lecturer made for himself. Arriving at the hall, they found it almost filled but managed to find three seats at the back.

The lecturer began by declaring that the material world in which we live is surrounded by invisible powers as real as anything we see or feel. Furthermore, he said, people should not be afraid of that which they cannot see, for the unseen forces are friendly and eager to help us. Our unbelief makes it impossible to know fully and to appreciate what is actually happening. "Death," he said, "is not really death as most people think of it; it is rather our entrance into the invisible world."

Pausing, he looked slowly over his audience and said: "Among the many newcomers here tonight are a lady and gentleman who arrived from Cape Town, South Africa, on April 6." He pointed to the back row.

"Their name is coming through now," he said. "Yes, a Mr. and Mrs. John R—."

This was the very couple that had come with some misgivings. Their faces were a study in amazement as the lecturer continued: "Less than six weeks ago the beloved sister of Mrs. R— passed over to the other side." Without hesitation he added: "In this

16

morning's mail Mrs. R— received a long airmail envelope with a letter and an enclosed snapshot of her sister."

"How on earth could he know that?" the lady whispered.

Continuing, he said: "This picture was taken on a beach at Cape Town two days prior to her death, which was the result of an automobile accident. And furthermore, Mrs. R— has that picture with her now. It is in the right-hand pocket of her brown handbag!"

With trembling hands the lady opened her bag. Sure enough, the photo and the letter were there. Surprised beyond belief, she took out the letter and the picture which had arrived that morning.

"And how do I know these things?" he continued. "Because, madam, your sister is standing right here beside me! She is on the platform at this very moment!"

Unbelievable, you say? But it happened! Then the lecturer began to convey a few comforting messages, each laden with personal information known only to these two sisters, one of whom had been buried five and a half weeks earlier.

The lady and her husband were no longer skeptical. They were sure there is an invisible world. No one could persuade them otherwise. The evidence was overwhelming. But what explanation can we give? It is easy to label it "clairvoyance," "telepathy," or "paranormal cognition." But that does not explain it. Those are mere words, not explanations. And scores of experiences could be cited. What would you have thought if something like that had happened to you?

University Student Converses With Spirits

Let me give you another brief chapter out of my own life. I was just twenty-one when I had my first real contact with spiritualism. A young man two years my senior, a university student from Birmingham, England, was called to serve in the same publishing house where I worked. He was a gifted writer and entertainer and in addition an outstanding athlete. He had a refreshing sense of humor and was anything but a visionary. We soon became fast friends. He made a confidant of me and told me about his past life.

He had served for a short time as assistant secretary for one of England's leading scientists, who was also a prominent spiritual-

ist. It is interesting to note in passing that men like Sir William
Crookes, Sir Oliver Lodge, and Sir Arthur Conan Doyle of an earlier generation, and Professor H. H. Price, Professor C. D. Broad,
and Dr. Raynor Johnson of more recent times are men who have
distinguished themselves as scientists, philosophers, and astrono-
mers, and are also devotees of spiritualism of one kind or another.

While working for this scientist, this young friend of mine met
many prominent people, a number of whom encouraged him in
the study of the occult science. Having lost both his mother and
sister by death, he readily turned to the teachings of spiritualism
for comfort. When a medium informed him that "departed ones"
were trying to get in touch with him, he freely opened his mind for
communication. From then on he had regular visits from apparitions purporting to be his mother and his sister. This was prior to
his leaving for Australia, where I met him and where he later came
under the conviction that spiritualism is condemned by the Bible
and that he should have nothing more to do with these apparitions. As a result of that conviction he rejected the spiritualistic
practice of years and turned his back upon all that pertained to it.

Apparitions in the Room

To disentangle himself was not easy, as anyone knows who has
tried. "I just cannot get away from the spirits," he told me.
"These apparitions won't leave me alone. They continually visit
me and tell me they are deeply wounded by my attitude. They
wake me up in the dead of night, sometimes three or four times a
night. What can I do to get away from it all?"

We were living not far from each other, so we decided it might
help if we shared a room. I could at least be company for him, and
I might be able to support him in his battle with the spirits. We put
our beds fairly close together, so that if he was troubled in the
night he could easily waken me.

All went well for a week or two. Both of us enjoyed athletics,
and we also read the classics together. Soon, however, he was
accosted by the same beings as before, and it happened as usual in
the middle of the night. First they would shake his bed to awaken
him. Then they would start to converse. They were usually semi-
transparent in appearance. One of them, he claimed, was the "liv-

ing image" of his mother, and in an audible voice this apparition would tell him of her affection for him. When he would say, "I do not believe you," and would turn his back, then the other, purporting to be his sister, would come to the other side of the bed and tell him he was breaking his mother's heart. When this happened he would switch on the light and begin to read. He always kept a devotional book or two handy.

All would be quiet for perhaps half an hour. Then suddenly the book would be snatched from his hands and flung to the other end of the room. The light would go out of its own accord, and a voice, harsh and strident, would call out, "You'll read, will you?"

Unusual you say? Yes, and a bit unnerving. About the only thing to do was to get up, dress, and go out into the clear air of the night. A long walk offered some respite. As young men we tried to think the whole thing through, but it was not easy. We felt the need of help from a higher source, so we prayed. And God heard our prayers, for deliverance came at last.

Those early experiences no doubt gave me some preparation for the more serious encounters related in the first chapter of this book.

Spiritism in the South Pacific

I am writing this while making another visit to the South Pacific Islands. Spirit worship and demon possession are vital parts of life in many of these areas, and no eyebrow is raised if an apparition appears or someone becomes demon possessed. They speak of spirits as they would of ordinary people, and some of these spirit activities seem to defy explanation. If you have never seen a person demon possessed, you might find it hard to believe what I am about to relate. Many reliable witnesses will substantiate this account. And remember, this did not happen fifty years ago, or twenty, or ten. It happened while this chapter was being written.

A young Fijian woman living in Winembuka, about sixty miles from Suva, whose grandfather had been a devil priest, decided she would try to contact the power with whom he communed. This was to be just a bit of fun, so she thought.

Unknown to her parents, she went out to the edge of the village and in her own strange way summoned the spirits. It soon became known that she was having these interviews. Her parents and friends who were Christians tried to reason with her, urging her to break from it, for they knew the character of these powers. But nothing they could say seemed to affect this young woman. The spirit with whom she was communing appeared not as a human being, but in the form of a great green snake* which she claimed lived at the far edge of the village in a water hole.

Possessed by a Demon

Against her parents' pleadings, this girl continued to have contact with this demon. Soon the whole community knew what was happening. It became so gruesome, even to her, that at last she realized she must make a break. One day she summoned all her mental strength and turned her back on the whole thing.

Then something happened! She immediately became possessed. Her appearance changed, and she would neither eat nor drink. Clearly a superhuman power controlled her. Thinking she would come out of the spell, the family let her remain in that state for a few days. Then in desperation they sent for their minister. After hearing the full story, this Christian leader asked two or three other ministers to join him. Together they sought God's power for the girl's deliverance.

Then they came to the home and endeavored to talk with this young woman, but she would not communicate. Instead, she became enraged and screamed defiance, threatening them. In reply they ordered the spirit, in the name of Jesus Christ, to come out of her. Suddenly she fastened her eyes upon them, glaring like a trapped animal. She dropped to the floor and, stretching out full length, with staring eyes and frothing mouth she made her way across the floor slithering like a snake. Then she became limp and completely still. They waited quietly for a few minutes, then bathed her face and gave her time to come to herself. At last she opened her eyes and sat up.

"Where am I, and why are you all here?" she asked, puzzled. To her surprise, they informed her that she had taken neither food nor water for three days.

Turning to her parents, she asked forgiveness for her defiance of their counsel. Then she thanked the ministers for their prayers, but most of all she gave gratitude to her Lord for her deliverance.

The minister who actually commanded the spirit to leave this young woman, had himself been reared in a home where demonism was practiced. His grandmother had been something of a devil priestess. Spiritism was part of her very life. However, the spirits helped her in a very practical way, providing her with all the money she needed for the home. Whatever money she spent at the store for food or clothes would always be restored to her, the exact amount always being in her purse when she returned home. This had gone on regularly for many years, as the neighbors well knew.

"That Trunk Is Taboo"

Her power seemed to be bound up with a trunk she kept locked in her bedroom. From his earliest years, this grandson had been warned he must never open it. "That trunk is taboo," his grandmother said. Being an obedient boy, he honored her instructions.

The spirit with whom she communed was just as real to her as any person in human flesh, and eventually this boy began to have experience with spirits himself. Even on the playground at school he would suddenly break away from the children and talk to someone. They would hear him calling out, and then he would run over and appear to spring up on someone's lap. No person was visible, but the lad would talk and appear to caress some personality, all the while being *suspended in midair*.

The children on the playground, as well as the teacher, had seen this happen many times. His association with this unseen personality would last a quarter of an hour or more. They would see him talking just as a child would to an adult. They often watched as he would lay his head back as if on someone's breast. And we repeat, all of this in midair!

When the interview was over he would slip quietly to the ground as if being helped by someone, and go on playing with the children. This occurred so often that nobody took notice of it. It is difficult for most of us to realize that such a thing could happen, but in certain areas of the world such occurrences are so common that they are taken for granted.

At the mission school this boy learned to pray and to look to

God for help and protection. After a time he refused to have contact with the spirits, much to his grandmother's distress. She became angry and threatened him, but she did not take him away from the school. Relating these experiences to me later, he mentioned how strange it was to live in a home where two powers were so definitely at work—the power of God and the power of demons.

He left that area to further his education at a Christian college not far from Suva. He later entered the ministry, and every day he prayed that God would give him wisdom to convert his grandmother whom he so dearly loved. When visiting her he tried to reason with her, but to no avail.

One day while on a short visit to the old home, he decided he would see what was in that old trunk his grandmother guarded so carefully. He felt he could never help her while she put her confidence in devil charms. This was a good opportunity, for she had gone to make some purchases. Opening the trunk, he found a little locked box. Finding the key, he opened it, and there were the objects he had expected to find. Now what was he to do? Put them back into the trunk? No! He felt it was now or never! So he took the whole thing and threw it into the river. Then he commanded the demon never to return to that home.

The Demon Power Leaves

As soon as the grandmother returned home, she sensed something was wrong. Going to her trunk, she sought for her little box with the charms. The box was gone! Going to her grandson, by then an ordained minister, she asked if he had been in her room.

"Yes," he said.

"Did you open that taboo trunk?"

"Yes!"

"Well, what happened to the little box in there? I can't find it."

"I threw it away, and I have prayed that the spirits will never come back into this home again."

Poor woman! She was almost too scared to look at him. "What will become of me now?" she asked in consternation.

He sat down quietly with her and read from the Scriptures. Still afraid, she knelt with him in prayer while he sought the power of he living God. She joined in that prayer, opening her heart to God and in her own simple way claiming His power to overcome the spirits. A few months later he had the joy of baptizing her and welcoming her into the church.

To tamper with the box of charms had seemed to her to be the unpardonable sin until she realized that the God of love was stronger than the god of fear.

Spirit powers are at work in many lands—in the largest cities of the world, in tiny villages in the South Seas, among the peoples of Central Africa, as well as in the cultural centers of Southern Asia and the Far East. The terminology is different in each of these areas, yet the philosophy is the same. One who has seen these powers at work can never doubt the phenomena. But to know their ultimate destiny, one must know their origin and something of their history. That is the theme of this book.

---

*In the sixteenth chapter of Acts we have the story of the young woman who was "possessed of a spirit of divination," verse 16. The marginal reading is "python." Geoffry Parrinder tells us "this was said originally to mean one who spoke through the power of the oracle of Delphi which was embodied in a python," or a snake. *Witchcrafts European and African* (Barnes and Noble, Inc., 1963). In the previous chapter we noted that spirits sometimes appear in the form of animals.

The New Look of the Occult

Occult science is not new. It is hoary with age. Ancient inscriptions have been found indicating the belief of the Akkadians in ghosts and the worship of spirits. In ancient times the influence of spirits was tremendous. Then during the middle ages of the Christian era it again came to the fore. But with the coming of the sixteenth-century Reformation it suffered a severe setback.

Now a change has come. The crudities of earlier days contrast strangely with the scientific approaches of our day. Modern spiritualism began in the humble home of the Fox family in Hydesville, near Rochester, New York, in 1848. The girls of this family, hearing strange noises, decided to get some response if possible. Snapping her fingers and rapping on the wall, Kate Fox called out, "Here, old Splitfoot, do this!" Back came the answer in the identical number of raps. This was repeated over and over again. Soon they began to get answers to questions, and this revealed to them that an intelligence was responsible for the rappings.

When the news broke, it awakened interest not only throughout America, but also in some of the most conservative countries of Europe. From this somewhat crude beginning it has developed until today spiritualism appeals to thinkers and influential leaders in many lands. In earlier days it wanted no part with the church. But there is a significant shift from the anti-Christian stand of a few decades ago to its pro-Christian attitude today. One now hears the term "Christian spiritualism."

A few years ago in London, England, we were holding evangelistic meetings in a large public hall. In a smaller hall attached to the same building a spiritualist group met every Sunday evening. At the conclusion of our services our audience had to pass the entrance to this smaller hall, and we heard that group singing some of the same Christian hymns we had been singing. Their prayers, of course, were different. While they used some of the same expressions we did, yet those prayers were not addressed to God, in the name of Jesus Christ. They were addressed to the spirits.

Spiritualism is no longer confined to the darkened rooms of other days. It has emerged from the shadowy alley and now seeks the bright lights of Broadway. It is rooted in the faith of millions. It claims to encompass in its philosophy all the mysteries of life, death, and eternity.

Spirit Healing and Hypnosis

Occult science, or spiritualism, is reaching out to areas other than religion. It is moving into medical circles and influencing medical techniques. Some surgeons are turning to hypnosis and discarding older methods of anesthesia, claiming that hypnosis has many advantages to both patient and doctor. Quite a few universities require their medical students to show proficiency in these methods before being graduated.

We are well aware that physicians, psychiatrists, and dentists who practice hypnosis would object to any accusation that this is related to occultism, much less spiritualism. We also recognize that hypnosis is about as old as humanity. Since its rediscovery in 1734 it has been much disputed. It was first known as mesmerism after the Vienna doctor, Anton Mesmer, reintroduced it into medical circles. At first considered quackery, it is now thought quite respectable and normal.

In London a duodenal ulcer was reportedly removed from a patient by a spirit entity purporting to be the discarnate spirit of a Dr. Reynolds who died more than a hundred years before. This materialized spirit worked at a surgical table. Ellaine Elmore, who was present and described the phenomenon, said, "The hands of the spirit seemed to disappear inside the patient's body." While performing the operation, the materialized spirit declared he would bring "the ulcer through a temporary hole in the stomach."

After the ulcer had been removed, it was sent to a laboratory in Manchester and identified as "an acute duodenal ulcer." The medical authority performing the analysis certified it as being an acute ulcer and commented on the evident "freshness of the tissue and also the fact that there was no trace of modern surgical methods having been used."

From very ancient times "spiritual healing," sometimes called "magnetic healing," has been known and practiced. Today it is assuming a major role. In the *Spiritualistic Manual*, page 116, we learn that magnetic healing "is now a tenet of the religion of spiritualism and is practiced among spiritualists in conformity with their religious belief and knowledge of the power of spiritual agencies."

Harry Edwards of Britain, a foremost spiritualist healer whose crowds have often filled to capacity the giant Royal Albert Hall in London, told investigators recently: "I am nothing. This is beyond the wisdom of man. . . . We couldn't work without the spirit friends. . . . It is all by the power of spirits that these changes take place."—*Into the Unknown*, page 127.

This man Harry Edwards has his "little sanctuary" at Burrows Lea near Guildford and is visited by five to six thousand people every year. In 1958 he received no less than 673,445 requests for healing, and he claims to have to his credit some thirty thousand paranormal healings.

Strange things are happening these days, things that demand investigation and frequently defy comprehension. We read the universe through different eyes from those of our grandfathers. Many things which were once regarded as the outworking of special providence are now recognized as being the result of scientific principle.

New understanding of the physical sciences is giving us new outlooks on our planet and its neighbors, and new insights into the natural world. Remarkable advances have also been made in the fields of mental science. Telepathy, clairvoyance, and paranormal cognition (extrasensory perception), once looked upon as the pastime of the ignorant, are today regarded as legitimate fields for scientific investigation.

Institutions of learning such as Duke University in North Carolina, the University of Utrecht in Holland, and the Freiburg University in Germany, have established professorships in parapsychology for the study of extrasensory perception, known as ESP. Even the Russians, usually regarded as definitely materialistic, have entered this field of scientific research.

Professor Leonid Vasiliev, of Leningrad University, who for some forty years has been probing this phenomenon, has reached some definite conclusions. The professor says that "suggestion at a distance—which is not affected by either distances or the curve of the earth—is affected, not by ordinary electromagnetic waves, but by some other, as yet unknown, form of energy."—Douglas Hunt, *Exploring the Occult*, 1964, page 106.

The Big Question

The big question is: What is this "yet unknown form of energy"? To doubt the phenomena or the facts of telepathy is foolish. But whether it be classified as in the *Encyclopaedia Britannica* under such headings as "telepathy, clairvoyance, lucidity, premonition, transutterance, xenoglossy, psychometry, or dramatic writing," or by anyone of a dozen other names, in each of these there is the possibility of real deception. We do not say this from prejudice, but because of experience. That which we are about to relate in this chapter should bring vividly to the reader what we mean.

Before citing definite cases, let us quote from Douglas Hunt, who as an occultist states the case very clearly. He says: "We saw that many people are turning to the occult interpretation of the universe because they no longer find materialism satisfactory. For them occultism becomes a way of life. They may have widely differing views, but on certain fundamentals practically all would agree.

"They would agree that the universe did not come into existence by accident, and they therefore accept the existence of a Plan, and assume that this implies a Planner. . . .

"In a way the Occultist is the only genuine materialist, for he believes that matter and substance are but opposing poles of the same cosmic root substance. For him, therefore, everything is matter, or, if you like to put it another way, everything is spirit. . . .

"One final tenet is probably common to almost all Occultists— the belief that something connected with ourselves survives death."—*Ibid.*, pp. 14, 15. Then he declares that one's "expansion of consciousness is merely a hastening of the process of evolution, from cave man to Archangel, in which every Occultist believes."—*Ibid.* "All life," occultists say, "is a process of evolution," while "death is not death, but another advanced life." This is a basic teaching of most Eastern religions and is the foundation on which spiritualism is built. And it is important to note that spiritualists are of necessity evolutionists, for their philosophy is that we are all in the process of development.

In the *Encyclopaedia Britannica,* fourteenth edition, article entitled "Spiritualism," we read of "a growing persuasion on the part of certain people that the activity of human beings is not entirely limited to the use they make of their bodily or material organisms on this planet. It is held that . . . an individuality can continue long after the temporary material body is worn out or otherwise resolved into its elements; . . . and shall be able under certain limitations to guide and influence terrestrial affairs in cooperation with those still living on earth. This may be taken roughly as the spiritualistic interpretation or explanation of certain obscure phenomena which have occurred sporadically from time immemorial, and which may be said to constitute the phenomena of spiritualism."

The article goes on to state that the subject "at the present time is a debatable one, on which there are many more or less legitimate differences of opinion." Yet, it continues, "there is a general consensus of agreement among those who have devoted time and attention to the subject that some of the phenomena are genuine."

Advances in Parapsychology and Telepathy

Research in the field of parapsychology is now a part of the curriculum in a number of universities. Mention has already been made of Duke University, North Carolina, which has been specializing in this for many years. As far back as 1943 Professor J. B. Rhine and his colleagues published the results of ten years' work on Psychokinesis (PK) and also Extrasensory Perception (ESP).

They claim that "foolproof laboratory methods" are being followed, and that it will not be long before spiritist phenomena will have been fully established and placed on a sound scientific basis. Parapsychology is regarded by some as the spiritual enlightenment for today, and many believe that this change in attitude and emphasis "is destined to be as profound as the Reformation of the sixteenth century."

Alson Smith declares: "The most immediate and obvious significance of parapsychology is in the field of medicine. . . . Consciously directed clairvoyance may now rival the X-ray machine in diagnostic importance and consciously directed psychokinesis may now permit the tremendous energy locked up in the mind to be used to heal the body."—*Religion and the New Psychology* (Garden City, New York: Doubleday and Co., Inc., 1951), page 155.

Waldamar Kaempffert expresses the same belief: "Parapsychology ought to become the most important of all sciences."

Reginald M. Lester asserts that "certain scientists are now working upon a new field of research, to harness supersonic rays, by means of which it is hoped to establish electronic communication with the spirit world. . . . It is believed that, in the same way as Morse telegraphy evolved into radio speech and television pictures, in the future it should be possible for everyone to hear and see those on the Other Side, and even to obtain panoramic pictures of the spirit world."—*In Search of the Hereafter*, George C. Harrop and Co., Ltd., 1951, page 213.

Shaw Desmond, to whom we have already referred, says that the Christian religion will soon be the "religion of Psychics." "Religion and Science," he says, "will not only talk, but will talk together." In that day, he says, "the Atomic World will be riddled with the psychic, steered by the psychic."—*Psychic Pitfalls* (London: Rider and Co., 1954), pages 269, 270.

Spiritism Follows Popular Evangelistic Methods

In Great Britian, spiritualism, expressed in many occult manifestations, is very aggressive. Patterning after the methods of the gospel evangelist, it is making converts by tens of thousands. The largest halls are used as gathering places for tremendous crowds.

At these gatherings the display of startling phenomena silences the scoffer and challenges the Christian.

Healing meetings for the sick are a popular feature. Gordon Turner of the Greater London Healing Campaign conducts as many as thirty-two spiritualistic campaigns in that one city in a single year. These series, which last for a week or even longer, consist of nightly meetings. Each begins with a stirring song service followed by prayer. At least fifteen "healers" are usually present. It is claimed that not more than 5 percent of the audience are actually spiritualists. Many come from curiosity, and they soon become converts.

Such demonstrations as these, however, are not new. The ancient pagan world was full of such things. The goddess Isis is said to have openly manifested herself in her own apparition while she was performing cures. Demonology and sorcery prevailed in ancient Egyptian priestcraft, and these became the "nurse of civilization," according to Joseph Ennemoser.

The priests of that day attended more to the "practical uses of medicine" than the "observance of religion." Patients were brought to the Egyptian temples, and certain areas of the temples became an "inner sanctum for the sacred healing art." "That wonderful cures were often performed in the temples is an undisputed fact."—*The History of Magic*, translated from the German by William Howlett (London: Henry G. Bohn), Vol. 1, p. 353. "Priests were consecrated who practiced religion associated with the healing art."—*Ibid.*, p. 357. Modern spiritualistic healing, then, is really a psychic regression to an archaic age.

In recent years spiritualist or occult churches are springing up in many countries of the world. Modern spiritualism has become so well accepted that in most states "medium-ministers" have the right to officiate at marriages, baptisms, and burials. In New York City alone there are 200 such ministers. For seventy or eighty years spiritualistic meetings were held largely in halls, but today the trend is to establish churches.

Spiritualism is growing even faster in Europe than in the United States. Already more than 1,000 such churches can be found among Great Britian's 50,000,000 population.

There is wide divergence of opinion concerning spiritualism.

While many are convinced it is genuine, others call it devilish. A few still speak of it as trickery and sleight of hand. But no truly informed person will attempt to dismiss it thus.

Greber claims that spiritualism "is man's only path to the truth and is the shortest road that leads to God." Earlier writers were not so positive. W. E. Harvey, writing in *The Harbinger of Light* years ago, expressed the hope that "it *may be* the channel divinely selected for the manifestation of the purposes of the Most High." At the time he wrote, few churchmen knew or even wanted to know its teachings. But today the picture is entirely different. While a few years ago it entered the church by the back door, today it is occupying the pulpit.

Strange Words from a Christian Leader

Dr. W. R. Matthews, late dean of St. Paul's, London, said: "Spiritualism is a confirmation of the Christian faith." Strange words these from a church leader! But the dean's is not a lone voice; his is but the echo of a chorus of voices. The late archbishop of Canterbury, Dr. Cosmo Lang, apppointed a committee some years ago consisting of two archbishops and thirty-five bishops of the Church of England to "report upon the Christian faith in relation to spiritualism." The world waited eagerly for their findings. But the full report was never published officially, although a London newspaper later came out with what it claimed was the full report. A few sentences from this will show the direction of the thinking of these bishops. The report said in part:

"It is possible that we may be on the threshold of a new science, which will, by another method of approach, confirm us in the assurance of a world behind and beyond the world we see, and of something within us by which we are in contact with it. We could never presume to set a limit to means which God may use to bring man to the realization of spiritual life."—Quoted in "The Findings of Archbishop Lang's Committee on Spiritualism," reprinted from *Psychic News*.

In *The Church of England and Spiritualism*, a pamphlet put out by London's Psychic Press Ltd., other statements appear.

"None of the fundamental Christian obligations or values is in any way changed by our acceptance of the possibility of communication with discarnate spirits.

"Where these essential principles are borne in mind, those who have the assurance that they have been in touch with their departed friends may rightly accept the sense of enlargement and of unbroken fellowship which it brings. . . .

"There is no reason why we should not accept gladly the assurance that we are still in closest contact with those who have been dear to us in this life, who are going forward, as we seek to do ourselves, in the understanding and fulfillment of the purpose of God. . . .

"In general we need much more freedom in our recognition of the living unity of the whole church, in this world and in that which lies beyond death."

The Anglican Church is not alone in its investigation. Psychic phenomena have been under study by the General Assembly of the Church of Scotland. In 1920 a special committee was appointed. After a two-year inquiry Dr. Norman Maclean, an ex-moderator, declared:

"The church decided that psychical research was not contrary to the teachings of the Christian faith, and that members of the church were not forbidden to exercise their minds in this field."— Quoted in "The Findings of Archbishop Lang's Committee on Spiritualism."

Not All Church Leaders Agree

Not all church leaders shared those opinions, however. Indeed, there was sharp division among the Anglicans. Dr. William Temple, at that time archbishop of York, was one who did not agree with the majority report. He said: "I took a foremost part in urging that the report would not be published." The archbishop, one of the clearest thinkers of the whole question of man's condition in death, recognized that the belief of the majority on the survival of the soul is unscriptural. He also recognized that spirtualists deny the atonement of Jesus Christ. After he became the archbishop of Canterbury he was by no means silent on the issue.

One of America's most widely known and best-loved ministers is Dr. Norman Vincent Peale, of the Marble Collegiate Church,

New York. In the October issue of *The Reader's Digest*, 1953, an article appeared under the title, "There Is No Death," in which he expressed his definite belief in survival after death. He spoke affectionately of his mother's passing and declared that he communes with her quite frequently. Note his words:

"I firmly believe in the continuation of life after what we call death takes place. I believe there are two sides to the phenomenon known as death: this side where we now live and the other side where we shall continue to live." "The New Testament teaches the indestructibility of life."

To reinforce this belief he cites the experience of our Lord who after His crucifixion had a "series of disappearances and reappearances." Dr. Peale must surely have overlookd the fact that these "reappearances" were made after He was raised from the dead, not while His body was lying in the tomb. The Scripture clearly states that when the disciples entered the sepulcher they "found not the body of the Lord Jesus." And as they stood there sorely perplexed the angel said: "Ye seek Jesus of Nazareth, which was crucified: He is risen: He is not here: behold the place where they laid Him." Mark 16:6.

The tomb was empty and the place where His body had lain was bare. The women had not come to the tomb to commune with a disembodied spirit, but to embalm His lifeless body. We repeat, it was not a disembodied spirit that was disappearing and reappearing, but the Lord Himself—a resurrected Man. On that same evening He said: "Handle Me, and see; for a spirit hath not flesh and bones, as ye see Me have." Luke 24:39. The tomb was empty, but He Himself was there bodily among them.

The unanswerable argument of those first Christian preachers was that Jesus Christ had been raised from the dead. Speaking of Jesus of Nazareth, Peter in the very first public sermon said: "Him . . . ye have taken, and by wicked hands have crucified and slain: whom God hath raised up, having loosed the pains of death." Acts 2:23, 24.

To prove He was not a mere spirit, Jesus urged Thomas to examine the nail prints in His hands and feet and the spear wound in His side. The mighty truth which the apostles heralded to the world is centered in our Lord's bodily resurrection. But today that truth is being distorted and misrepresented, often by well-meaning people, some of them ministers.

We say this not in a spirit of challenge, much less in condemnation, but the article referred to in *The Reader's Digest* naturally creates confusion. And there will always be confusion as long as we try to harmonize the unscriptural teaching of Greek philosophy with the clear teaching of bodily resurrection, which is the message of Scripture revelation.

The fact that spiritualism now appears in clerical robes makes it the more deceptive. Some claim it is a science; others that it is a philosophy. But millions accept it as a religion, believing it to be the only true religion in the world. While spiritualism has decidely changed in outward appearance and method, yet its basic claims remain the same. Modern names do not change the nature of an ancient cult.

Spiritualism's Basic Claim Challenges God's Word

The Bible says: "The dead know not anything." Ecclesiastes 9:5. "His sons come to honor, and he knoweth it not; and they are brought low, but he perceiveth it not of them." Job 14:21. But spiritualism declares: "There is no death; there are no dead."— Mrs. M. E. Cadwallader, *Centennial Book*, page 68.

In the June, 1964, issue of *The Summit of Spiritual Understanding*, Clyde A. Dibble says: "We do not communicate with the dead but with the living. . . . The evidence is increasing that they are not silent and away, only that many are still blind, deaf, and insensitive spiritually to those other dimensions of the spirit." Dibble heads the "Lyceum Department" column of the journal.

In the same issue Arthur A. Meyers of the "Quiz Corner" states that "Infinite Intelligence is not a formulated divine creature." This infinite Power has been known as Jehovah, God, Spirit, Ra, and as the "Infinite Intelligence" of spiritualism. Continuing, this responsible interpreter of spiritualist beliefs says: "*You are the expression of Spirit Universal;* your body is the temple of Spirit; you are a child of God—Good—Harmony and Infinite Intelligence; *you are that Power.*" (Italics supplied.)

Here, then, is spiritualism's clear declaration that man makes himself God. This agrees exactly with the serpent's promise made to Eve in the Garden of Eden—"Ye shall not surely die: . . . ye shall be as gods." Genesis 3:4, 5. The question each must decide for himself is, Whom shall we believe, God or the devil? Our decision determines our destiny.

In recent years spiritualistic leaders seem eager to identify their movement with every form of religious phenomenon which could be used to bring the movement prestige. A current example is the claim by Robert J. Macdonald in his address to the officers, trustees, and delegates of the Seventy-Seventh Annual Spiritualist Convention. Among other things he said: "One of the newer phenomena in the field of religion is the interest in glossolalia [speaking in tongues] which has captured the interest of major Protestant sects. . . . When Modern Spiritualism came into being in 1848, a great many early mediums experienced this phenomenon and it has continued to some extent in our organization."—Quoted in *The Summit of Spiritual Understanding*, November, 1964. Perhaps his most significant observation is this: "No doubt glossolalia [tongues speaking] will be of great assistance to the merging groups."

R. J. Macdonald is the president of the movement, and his reference to glossolalia is deeply significant. This phenomenon is coming more and more to the front. Some Christian groups that a few years ago strongly opposed speaking in tongues have to face the fact today that it is being experienced by many of their members, including some prominent ministers.

It is not our purpose here to examine the origin and effects of glossolalia in the church, although much more needs to be understood on this. But we would simply point out that spiritualism, which for more than a century has given no place to this phenomenon, now seems eager to identify itself with this popular manifestation. Whether speaking in tongues will play a vital role in assisting the merging groups as this spiritualist leader says, time alone will tell.

Spiritualism's "new look" certainly differs from the "old look." The future of this movement will eclipse anything of the past.

Ghosts That Walk and Talk

From time immemorial ghosts and ghost stories have intrigued the human race. Here is a recent account of an occurrence in England:

"Parties of up to forty men, armed with shotguns and rifles, last night searched the woods around Saltwood, near Hythe, for a ghost. Villagers claimed they saw the ghost, in a red cloak carrying a lantern, near Slaybrook Corner, scene of an ancient battle. His appearance was preceded by mysterious lights and a 'ball of fire.' Some think the ghost may be that of a Roman soldier killed in the battle. Others say William Tournay, wealthy eccentric landowner who died sixty years ago, has come back to haunt the village. But whoever he is, he was too smart for the hunters last night. Nobody sighted him."—Quoted in the Sydney *Sun*, Australia, December 6, 1963.

Is all this imaginary, or do ghosts actually appear? Is there survival after death? There is scarcely a country or island anywhere in the world where witchcraft is not known. From the icy regions of the Ona in the southern tip of South America, to the Eskimos of northern Alaska, spirit worship is known and practiced.

Dr. Wendell Oswalt states in his recent book, *Napaskiah–An Alaskan Eskimo Community*, that the shamans among the Eskimos communicate with the spirit world to cure or create illness and disease, or prophesy the future. Their power results from association with the spirit of a deceased shaman.

He also emphasizes the important part women once played in the Eskimo community through their witchcraft. In a personal interview we asked Professor Oswalt if spirit worship was known in these parts before the introduction of any Christian influence.

"Unquestionably," he said. "All over the Western Hemisphere spirit worship was known. Some of the most ancient customs have their origin in either fear of, or reverence for, spirits."

The same claims can be made for the Australian aborigines. Magic and spirit worship play an awesome role among these primitives, and at times unbelievable things seem to happen. "The aborigines' world is peopled by spirits. Each man has his spirit; so have trees and rocks and animals. Spirit children wait for their fathers to dream of them before they can be born. The spirits of the dead sometimes manifest themselves. Magic impregnates places and things; there are taboos; it is easy to be 'caught' by some of the mysterious forces always about, or to be the victim of sorcery."—Ronald Rose, *Living Magic* (New York: Rand, McNally & Company, 1956).

During recent years a whole new vocabulary has been developed, particularly in the areas of occult science. The physical body is now spoken of as the "etheric husk" which, womb-like, nourishes the "astral body." This "astral body" or "etheric body," as it is also called, is claimed to be a duplicate of the physical body, except that it "knows no disfigurement," nor does it share "other defects so common to the physical body."

Expressions such as "incarnate," referring to the physical body, and "discarnate," referring to the so-called astral body, may have little or no meaning for some of us, but are familiar to an enlarging group. They speak glibly of the "seven planes" of existence, which Dr. Raynor Johnson lists as:

1. The Plane of Matter. . . . The Physical form. . . .

2. An Intermediate State. . . . Our "aetheric level."

3. The Plane of Illusion. More usually called the "astral" plane. . . . "Heaven."

4. The Plane of Colour. The highest plane of existence in human form. . . .

5. The Plane of Flame.

6. The Plane of White Light.

7. The Final State. Awareness of Ultimate Reality. Communion with the Supreme.—*Nursing of Immortality* (London: Hodder and Stouten, 1960), page 243.

Geraldine Cummins, in her book *Travellers in Eternity*, gives the following as a message from a "spirit":

"To me it seems as if I left you only four weeks instead of years ago. That is because when one is happy time flashes by like a falling star. . . . There is nothing to catch here—no trains or buses and no income tax collector or other nuisances. . . . I admit that I have had my bad depressing and painful hours since I left the earth, but out of them blossomed flowers of lovely life. . . . There are great cities over here for people who like cities. Harold has taken me on a short visit to Purgatory, which is another London. . . . But this etheric London isn't all purgatory. There are some lovely people living contentedly in small houses in rather grubby streets. They were good souls, but such streets were their idea of heaven, so they found it."—Pages 146, 147.

What were at one time considered mere hallucinations, unworthy of careful investigation, are now being taken seriously. Many claim that parapsychology will yet become "the most important of all sciences." Dr. Hereward Carrington, Director of the American Psychical Institute, declares, "Many of us regard psychical research as 'the most important work being done in the world today.' " And Shaw Desmond of England says that soon "we shall use our places of worship . . . for the demonstration of life after death, and that we shall find before us the Teacher and Priest combined in the etheric form, which will materialize before our unastonished eyes."—*Psychic Pitfalls,* page 269. ("Unastonished," because the phenomenon will be so common it will be taken for granted.)

Almost unbelievable experiments are under way in many countries to bring about communion with invisible powers. Many of these are being carried out, not in the dark séances of earlier years, but in broad daylight or under strong artificial lights. Often there are scores, even hundreds, of observers present, including scientists.

According to a report that appeared some years ago in *Time* magazine, "10,000,000 out of the 61,000,000 population in Brazil indulge in the spiritist cults." One demonstrator named Mirabelli does the most astounding things. Normally this man can converse in two or at most three languages. But when he passes into a state of trance he can discuss topics intelligently in as many as twenty different languages. He has written in twenty-eight languages! In exactly twenty minutes, he once produced in excellent Czecho-slovakian, nine pages on "The Independence of the Czech." On another occasion he wrote twenty-five pages in forty-five minutes in Iranian on the subject of "The Instability of the Greek Em-pire." On each of these occasions he was performing under the closest public scrutiny.

He also demonstrated in other remarkable ways, such as play-ing billiards without touching the cue. Once he completely van-ished from sight, leaving behind a group of witnesses at the São Paulo railway depot. He appeared two minutes later at São Vicente, twenty-five miles distant.

During a séance held in a laboratory in the city of Santos a child's voice was heard to call, "Papa." Among those investigat-ing were ten scientists, including a Dr. Sousa. He was deeply stirred by that child's voice, for he declared it was the voice of his own daughter. Taking this apparition in his arms, he assured those present that she was indeed his daughter lost by death. The ap-parition remained in full view of the group for more than thirty minutes. Another investigator also took "her" in his arms and asked a number of questions. The investigators declared that the replies were absolutely rational. At the close all ten scientists present signed a document confirming the truthfulness of the re-port.

Perhaps the most astounding of such experiences was the ap-pearance of "Bishop José de Carmango Barros." Everyone present knew that the real bishop had been shipwrecked some time before and was dead. He had been well-known in the com-munity. The unusual thing about this appearance was that the ap-parition came not as a translucent, ghostly figure, but was dressed in episcopal robes. A medical doctor present examined this ap-parition, "listened to his heart action and breathing, tapped the body, examined the teeth, rubbed his finger over his gums to as-certain the presence of saliva, checked his veins, his eyeballs, and his fingernails." Other witnesses present also checked him, and each was convinced that he had examined a being that possessed the organs of a normal human body.

Another Amazing Incident

"On January 5, 1939, seventeen-year-old Maria and her grandmother were passing a bridge where three years before the body of Giuseppe Veraldi had been found, apparently a suicide. Maria stopped still, stared at the riverbank, and fainted. When she regained consciousness, she spoke in a coarse, masculine voice. 'I am Pepe,' she said, and she began to drink wine and smoke cigarettes, play cards, and write in the handwriting of the dead Giuseppe Veraldi. She told how his friends had drugged his wine, and thrown him over the bridge, and beaten him to death with an iron pipe. Then she acted out the crime. Eventually she returned to her normal self when the dead boy's mother ordered 'him' to leave her. Twelve years later a letter came from one of Giuseppe Veraldi's cronies, now living in Argentina, confessing to the crime just as Maria had described it."—*Time*, "Ghost Stories," February 18, 1957.

Professor Charles Richet, a psychologist who has given over thirty years to the study of the human mind, has said that at last he is "reluctantly compelled to the spiritist conclusion that the ghost was a living being and did survive the death of the body." Richet's examination of apparitions was so thorough that, according to Shaw Desmond, "he weighed them, measured them, tested with the tourniquet their blood pressure, and generally did with them what anyone may do with the physical body of his friends."— *Psychic Pitfalls*, page 137.

The Lyceum Movement

We have already referred to the lyceum movement which has become one of the most influential movements in modern spiritualism. This is conducted somewhat on the order of a Sunday School, but it differs in some respects. Besides hymns and devotionals there is physical recreation and the practice of clairvoyance. One visitor remarked: "It is a most unusual experience to see hundreds of lyceum children crowd into a town hall

and sing earnestly the well-known song from our hymnbook,
'Perish policy and cunning, trust in God and do the right.' "

Juvenile minds naturally respond to phenomena of this kind.
One lad was asked, "Why do you like to learn to march?" He
replied, "So I can march with the spirit people." The stated objective of the spiritualistic lyceum movement is to "give young
minds the natural principles of spiritualism, so that when they
grow up they will come to it the natural way."

It is difficult to imagine the impact on a child's mind, when,
after telling the story of how his pet dog was killed six months
earlier, the boy suddenly looks around and there is "Prince" materialized. Bounding up to his little master, this dog apparition
performs all his favorite tricks. Do you think you could convince
the boy that it was not his dog at all? If spiritualism's claims are to
be settled simply by what one sees—if "seeing is believing"—
then the case is already closed. But dare we trust our sight alone?
Not all of our senses put together are sufficient to settle this question. Here we have something too important to be decided by
sight or hearing or touch. We must know where we stand.

The Adversary Unveiled

Psychic power, as we have already noted, is as old as the world. Philosophers, poets, religionists, and educators have all grappled with the problem of good and evil, of righteousness and sin, of man and his destiny. Every religion has some theory on the subject. Sometimes these principles of good and evil are personified and represented as being either in conflict or complementary to each other, as for example the yin and the yang of China. Spiritualist writers go even farther. Jane Sherwood says that to really understand the issue we must think of it not as "a fight between Good and Evil, but as a necessary balance of the opposing forces of order and disorder; of creativity and destruction."—*The Country Beyond*, page 136.

This writer actually makes God the author of evil. But she endeavors to clarify the situation by saying, "We do not know fully what is good and what is evil."—*Ibid*. These statements are not the writer's own words but rather quotations from her spirit guide. Continuing, she says: "In fact, the two poles of existence, the positive and the negative, are necessary to the existence of every entity, whether it is of matter alone, or of matter and ether, as in plant life; of matter, ether, and astral substance as in the animal; or of matter, ether, astral, and ego-being as in man. . . . Each new Eden has been in turn invaded by the old serpent. The earth and its etheric and astral planes are the great arena of this cosmic strife. . . . God . . . was powerless to segregate His own being, to parcel it out into separate living units, without the help of the alien principle of matter."—*Ibid*., pp. 136-138.

How empty such imaginings sound by comparison with the

Word of God. The apostle Paul comes to grips with the problem in his letters. He writes of dethroned powers and pictures them not as partners in God's creation but as enemies at war with the Christian church. "For our fight is not against human foes, but against cosmic powers, against the authorities and potentates of this dark world, against the superhuman forces of evil in the heavens." Ephesians 6:12, The New English Bible.

In the New Testament Christ is pictured as in the act of defeating these "powers," like a gladiator in the arena in full view of the public. And we can never understand the issues involved until we recognize that Christ at Calvary conquered the whole kingdom of darkness. "And then, having drawn the sting of all the powers ranged against us, He exposed them, shattered, empty and defeated, in His final glorious triumphant act!" Colossians 2:15, Phillips. The New English Bible reads: "He made a public spectacle of them and led them as captives in His triumphal procession."

Seven centuries before Paul, the prophet Isaiah saw in Babylon, "the oppressor," a symbol of the cosmic powers of evil. It is obvious he is not speaking of an earthly king of an ancient city when he says:

"How art thou fallen from heaven, O Lucifer, son of the morning! how art thou cut down to the ground, which didst weaken the nations! For thou hast said in thine heart, I will ascend into heaven, I will exalt my throne above the stars of God: I will sit also upon the mount of the congregation, in the sides of the north: I will ascend above the heights of the clouds; I will be like the Most High." Isaiah 14:12-14.

Who was this being called Lucifer? The name means "Light Bearer." Other scriptures reveal him as the leader of the angelic host. Strife, then, did not begin in some far corner of the universe, but in the very heart of a being who occupied a place next to God Himself. His high position should have made him humble; instead it made him proud. Filled with self-importance, he felt he could rule the universe better than God. He became disloyal and challenged the throne of Deity. Giving place first to pride, then to jealousy, then covetousness, this mighty angel at last led an open rebellion against the government of heaven.

In his famous speech to King Henry in Shakespeare's play, Wolsey says: "Fling away ambition, for by it fell the angels." This is no mere Shakespearian concept; it is a Scriptural truth. Unholy ambition knows no bounds. It will stop at nothing to accomplish its diabolical ends. Lucifer declared, "I will be like the Most High." But God said, "Thou shalt be brought down to hell." Verse 15.

In the book of Revelation we read: "War broke out in heaven. Michael and His angels waged war upon the dragon. The dragon and his angels fought, but they had not the strength to win, and no foothold was left them in heaven. So the great dragon was thrown down, that serpent of old that led the whole world astray, whose name is Satan, or the devil—thrown down to the earth, and his angels with him." Revelation 12:7-9, Phillips.

The titanic struggle between the dragon with his rebellious angels and Michael with His loyal angels resulted in the expulsion of the rebels from heaven. Peter says, "God spared not the angels that sinned, but cast them down to hell"—*Tartarus,* the Greek word for the regions of darkness. 2 Peter 2:4. Jesus said, "I beheld Satan as lightning fall from heaven." Luke 10:18.

Description of Lucifer

Ezekiel the prophet writes of another monarch, the king of Tyre, whose arrogance and pride were proverbial. Then, like Isaiah, he sees in this power the human expression of the unseen ruler of evil. While he does not actually use the name Lucifer, yet his description leaves no doubt as to his meaning.

"Son of man, take up a lamentation upon the king of Tyrus, and say unto him, Thus said the Lord God; Thou sealest up the sum, full of wisdom, and perfect in beauty. Thou hast been in Eden the garden of God; every precious stone was thy covering, the sardius, topaz, and the diamond, the beryl, the onyx, and the jasper, the sapphire, the emerald, and the carbuncle, and gold: the workmanship of thy tabrets and of thy pipes was prepared in thee in the day that thou wast created. Thou art the anointed cherub that covereth; and I have set thee so: thou wast upon the holy mountain of God; thou hast walked up and down in the midst of the stones of fire. Thou wast perfect in thy ways from the day that thou wast created, till iniquity was found in thee. By the multitude of thy merchandise they have filled the midst of thee with violence, and thou hast sinned: therefore I will cast thee as profane out of the mountain of God: and I will destroy thee, O covering cherub, from the midst of the stones of fire. Thine heart was lifted up because of thy beauty, thou hast corrupted thy wisdom by reason of thy brightness: I will cast thee to the ground, I will lay thee before kings, that they may behold thee. Thou hast defiled thy sanctuaries by the multitude of thine iniquities, by the iniquity of thy traffic; therefore will I bring forth a fire from the midst of thee, it shall devour thee, and I will bring thee to ashes upon the earth in the sight of all them that behold thee. All they that know thee among the people shall be astonished at thee: thou shalt be a terror and never shalt thou be anymore." Ezekiel 28:12-19.

Every phrase here is important. Note these statements: "Thou hast been in Eden the garden of God." There he played for big stakes and won the world. As "the anointed cherub" he had once stood by the very throne of God. He had "walked up and down in the midst of the stones of fire" in the presence of Deity. And now the indictment: "Thine heart was lifted up because of thy beauty, thou hast corrupted thy wisdom by reason of thy brightness." Verse 17. Pride and coruption walk hand in hand. Then having instilled the spirit of treachery among his fellow angels, he led a third of them in a war of rebellion.

War is a frightening thing, even to us human beings. But what must it be when spiritual beings go into battle! Just how these mighty powers fight is beyond human comprehension. But Scripture reveals the result: "The great dragon, . . . called the Devil, and Satan, . . . was cast out into the earth, and his angels were cast out with him"; "neither was their place found anymore in heaven." Revelation 12:9, 8. And Jude speaks of "the angels which kept not their first estate, but left their own habitation." These he declared are "reserved . . . unto the judgment of the great day." Jude 6.

To know the future of these unseen powers we must understand the purpose of the incarnation, when God became a man in the person of Jesus Christ. The Scriptures declare plainly that Christ came to "destroy the works of the devil." 1 John 3:8. He came to dispossess the prince of evil of the kingdom he claimed. Christ therefore met the devil in a frontal attack. A tremendous conflict raged around Him. Even as a tiny Babe, Jesus was exposed to the workings of this sinister foe. When King Herod passed a decree demanding the slaughter of the infants (Matthew 2:16), his purpose was to destroy Christ as soon as He was born. This all-out war against the purpose of God and His plan to save the world, is vividly portrayed in Revelation, chapter 12.

Yet in spite of all the devil's efforts, the Child was born and grew to manhood. Before He began His ministry as a great Teacher, however, Jesus met the devil face to face. By various subtleties and temptations the devil tried to overcome Him. At one time Satan caused "all the kingdoms of the world" to pass before Christ in panoramic glory. And Satan said, "All this power will I give Thee, and the glory of them: for that is delivered unto me; and to whomsoever I will I give it." Luke 4:6.

Jesus did not dispute his claim, but simply stated: "It is written, Thou shalt worship the Lord thy God, and Him only shalt thou serve." Verse 8. Had Christ obeyed the great deceiver, He would have followed the example of the first man Adam, and could never have been the world's Saviour. Both Satan and Christ knew that. And it was a terrible blow to the prince of evil when the Prince of Peace refused.

Dethroned Powers

The issue came to its terrific climax at Calvary. Here the King of love and the king of hate met in mortal combat. Through those dark and agonizing hours Jesus struggled against the combined powers of hell. On that bald hill outside Jerusalem the conflict of the ages reached its most desperate height. But in spite of all the devil could do, the Saviour of the world held to the principles of righteousness and won a glorious victory. That crucial cry from the cross, "It is finished," was no moan of despair; it was a shout of triumph. Finished indeed was the contest for the ownership of this world.

That mighty shout, "It is finished," which rang from Calvary's hill, sounded the death knell of Satan and his hosts. The battle had been won, the enemy unmasked, and the king of hell dethroned.

And it was the Creator Himself who descended to the battlefield of earth and broke the stranglehold of evil.

When Jesus died it was no mere human sacrifice; it was God offering Himself for lost men. Having died in the place of man, He became the Redeemer of the lost race. At the completion of that sacrifice, a mighty shout was heard in heaven: "Now is come salvation: . . . for the accuser of our brethren is cast down." Revelation 12:10.

That song of praise from the angelic host reverberated to the very periphery of the universe. The battle had been won, assuring us that evil will ultimately be eradicated from the universe. But in the meantime the conflict between truth and error, between the kindgom of light and the kingdom of darkness, has continued and will continue until our Lord returns in glory. Then the devil and his hosts will be overthrown.

Is Occultism Christian?

Spiritualistic phenomena have been known and practiced from the earliest times, usually under the name of witchcraft. Modern spiritualism, however, arose about the middle of the ninetenth century and soon attracted national attention. During recent decades it has spread like an epidemic, and today it claims a membership of some 60,000,000. No longer is it associated with the darkened séance of wizardry and witchcraft; it now basks in the spotlight of scientific investigation, claiming world attention.

The advocates of this movement make tremendous claims for its future. As Ernest Thompson states "Spiritualism is a divine revelation, . . . a flood of light revealing the path to truth, love, justice, and peace."—*The Teachings and Phenomena of Spiritualism*, page 93.

The *Spiritualist Manual*, recognized voice of the cult, declares in its ninth revision, 1955, "It is the mission of spiritualism to revolutionize the world, to sweep away the accumulated rubbish of centuries of ignorance and superstition."—Page 79.

Among the teachings this spiritualist book calls "accumulated rubbish" are many of the basic doctrines of Christianity such as the return of Christ as Judge, the resurrection of the dead, the cleansing of the earth from sin and rebellion. "The Christian-Orthodox Church associates death with a Judgment Day when at the general resurrection on the last day 'we shall be changed in a moment.' Spiritualism breaks with orthodox belief and asserts that heaven and hell are purely states of consciousness which can as easily be manifest with us on earth as in a future existence."—*The Teachings and Phenomena of Spiritualism*, page 87.

Then, emphasizing the place spiritualism, or modern occultism, is to play in the immediate future, Thompson says: "The mission of spiritualism is to save mankind from the abyss of materialism to which he is now proceeding. Spiritualism has a mighty mission to fulfill, and spiritualists are missionaries of this new teaching of the so-called 'Christ spirit.' "—*Ibid.*, p. 72.

Following the trend of all spiritualist writers, he declares that "the teachings of spiritualism are basically the same as the teachings of Jesus." But having said that, he proceeds to undermine this by claiming that spiritualism has "a new and more enlightened foundation in the accumulation of nearly 2000 years of scientific and philosophic wisdom. The message of spiritualism is more advanced," he says, "insofar as its appeal is fashioned for the ears of educated people of a scientific age. Scientific materialism has vanquished orthodox religion, and therefore the only religion which can possibly take its place must have a scientific substructure. And spiritualism is such a religion. The basis of spiritualism is demonstrated survival and its philosophical superstructure is eternal progress."—*Ibid*.

What is this new and more enlightened foundation "that has vanquished orthodox religion"? Does it have anything in common with biblical Christianity? We will let the leaders of spiritualism give the answer.

Christ's Atoning Sacrifice Rejected

Sir Arthur Conan Doyle, whose work has already been noted, does not hesitate to state that the teachings of spiritualism and Christianity cannot be harmonized. Speaking for the movement, he declares, "The organized Spiritualist does not accept vicarious atonement nor orginal sin, and believes that a man reaps what he sows with no one but himself to pull out the weeds."—*Wanderings of a Spiritualist*, page 24, 25.

He says further: "One can see no justice in the vicarious sacrifice, nor in the God who could be placated by such means. [How grossly he misconstrues grace and atonement!] Above all, many cannot understand such expressions as the 'redemption from sin,' 'cleansed by the blood of the Lamb,' and so forth. . . . Never was there any evidence of a fall. But if there was no fall, what became of the atonement, of the redemption, or original sin, or a large part of Christian mystical philosophy?'' —*Cosmopolitan*, January, 1918, page 69.

He also predicted: "Spiritualism will sweep the world and make it a better place in which to live. When it rules over all the world, *it will banish the blood of Christ.*" (Italics supplied.)

To a Christian, such a statement is blasphemy. But expressions of this kind are not unusual in spiritualistic literature.

Sir Oliver Lodge, noted British scientist and a contemporary of Sir Arthur, expressed similar ideas. He says: "I believe the Christ is a great and wonderful personality. . . . He was sent to be man's example for all time . . . and to prove the individual continuity of life after death. *But He did not come to save men from the results of their sins.*"—*Claude's Book*, page 41. (Italics supplied.)

Converse E. Nickerson, prominent spiritualist minister and writer, in an article published in the November, 1964, issue of *The Summit of Spiritual Understanding*, also attacks the atonement. He writes: "Within the compass of consciousness dwells all our hope of eternal life. Such a life cannot be bought with the idle tenets of a religion based on an appeasement figured in a blood-atonement of an innocent man. Crafty theologians of that early day which immediately followed the closing life of the Master of Nazareth—called the Christ—seized upon the dramatic setting of Calvary to proclaim Jesus the 'atoning sacrifice' whose shed blood would blot out all our iniquities."—Page 4.

That there has been no change in spiritualistic doctrines is also evident from this statement by Ernest Thompson: "We definitely and firmly repudiate the idea that Jesus and His supreme sacrifice on the cross can save us. . . . To us the idea that 'He died that we might be forgiven' or that our sins can be forgiven by repentance or a priestly absolution is to create a conception of life's responsibilities which tends to encourage the wrongdoer in his way."—*The Teachings and Phenomena of Spiritualism*, page 84.

Christ's Virgin Birth

The militant spirit of this movement is revealed in many ways, but nowhere is it more evident than in its attacks upon the cardinal beliefs of Christianity. The "virgin birth" of Christ is an example. Converse E. Nickerson, like others before him, ridicules the virgin birth of Jesus. He says: "By no stretch of the imagination could this prophecy (Isaiah 7:14) be applied to Jesus the son of Joseph and Mary. . . . These are invented fancies that the early church fathers inserted into this Gospel according to Matthew. It is on the face of it a base forgery. . . . The miraculous birth of Jesus rests upon impossible testimony." Continuing, he claims that "Paul denies the virgin birth . . . and emphasizes the carnal origin of Mary's son and places the paternity definitely with Joseph, her husband. Paul never heard of any miraculous intervention concerning the birth of Jesus the Nazarene."—*The Summit of Spiritual Understanding*, October, 1964, page 4.

This writer then condemns the prophet Isaiah whose prediction concerning the miraculous birth of our Lord is so definitely endorsed by the Holy Spirit in the opening chapter of the New Testament. He not only ridicules the miraculous birth of Jesus, but charges Isaiah with being party to duplicity, who in order to make his own prediction come true actually sets out to either "find a girl with child or make her so"! Then, to "show the imposition and falsehood of Isaiah," he claims the incident is "passed over in silence." He closes his article with these words: "Thus much for the prophet Isaiah, and the book that bears his name."

The Interrupted Meeting

Some years ago I was addressing a large audience in London on the subject "Who Are the Spirits in Spiritism? Can We Talk With the Dead?" Hundreds of spiritualists were present, among them some prominent leaders of the movement. During the presentation I read publicly some forthright statements from their writings.

As I finished reading from a certain book, I noticed a well-dressed lady rise to her feet. She had been seated in the front row of the dress circle. Noticing that she continued to stand, I paused and asked if she desired to say something.

"Yes," she said, "I disagree with what you say. You claim that spiritualists are not Christians. I say they are."

"Well," I said, "before replying I would like to know to whom I am speaking. Would you care to give me your name?"

"Certainly," she said. "My name is Estelle Roberts."

"The Estelle Roberts who for so many years acted as medium for Sir Arthur Conon Doyle?" I asked.

"Yes," she replied, "I am the one."

"Well, I am glad you are here," I said. "You should be in a position to know the literature of spiritualism. Perhaps you would tell this audience if this book [the one I was holding] is authentic." I gave the title and the publisher.

She readily agreed it was one of the spiritualists' recognized and authoritative works. Then after reading one or two more statements of this kind I said: "This is evidently what the author wished his readers to understand. Don't you think so?"

"Yes, I suppose it is," she replied. "I had forgotten that part. I am sorry for the interruption."

Actually I was glad for the interruption, for it confirmed what I had been saying. And the confirmation came from Miss Estelle Roberts, who was and still is rcognized as "one of the greatest mediums and possessor of nearly every psychic faculty."—*This Is Spiritualism*, page 30.

Spiritualists Refused to Be Called Christians

One of the most representative of spiritualistic journals is the *Progessive Thinker*, edited for a time by Mrs. M. E. Cadwallader of the National Spiritualist Association. As far back as 1920 this statement appeared in this authoritative publication: "We refuse to be called by the name of Christian Spiritualist, because the word Christian stands for the dogma of salvation by man's death, a blood atonement. While we gladly accept many beautiful things as taught by Christ, we cannot afford to call ourselves Christian, for that would imply that we believe His blood really cleanses from sin; and we deny this. Spiritualism is a religion, but it is a religion free from the absurd and superstitious features that mar the system known as Christianity."

Attacking the so-called "objectionable features" of the Christian message, this same writer said: "I denounce the following: the vicarious atonement, the doctrine of eternal punishment, the literal resurrection of the body, the virgin birth of Jesus, the infallibility of the Bible, the doctrine of salvation by faith only. No, the spiritualist religion is as different from the so-called

Christian religion as a sunny day is from a starless night."

This writer's contrast is significant, but it is Christianity that is the "sunny day" and spiritualism the "starless night."

It may come as a surprise to many that spiritualism openly attacks the doctrines of Christianity. Actually the spiritualist philosophy is the antithesis of the Christian message. This is reemphasized in Ernest Thompson's *The History of Modern Spiritualism*, where he says, "Our spiritual progress is only the net result of our own efforts, and our sins cannot be forgiven or remitted by the vicarious atonement of a Saviour."—Page 12.

In his book, *The A.B.C. of Spiritualism*, issued by the National Spiritual Association of Churches, Dr. B. F. Austin answers a vital question: "Does Spiritualism recognize Jesus as one person of the Trinity, coequal with the Father, and divine in a sense in which divinity is unattainable by other men?" The unequivocal answer is: "No. Spiritualism accepts him as one of many savior christs, who at different times have come into the world to lighten its darkness and show by precept and example the way of life to men. It recognizes him as a world savior, but not as 'that only name' given under heaven by which men can be saved."—Question 17.

Need we quote more from spiritualist writings to show that they are not only non-Christian, but anti-Christian?

As if Christianity depended for its success upon salaried ministers, Ernest Thompson says, "The specter of spiritualism is haunting parish priests because it means death to their dogmas and a struggle for stipends, consequently they attack us." Then he says, "This opposition must be overcome by constant propaganda, education, organization, and a militant spirit of certain victory."—*The Teachings and Phenomena of Spiritualism*, page 101. Such statements leave no room for misunderstanding.

Misquoting Scripture

Now note the loose way spiritists quote and misquote Scripture. While claiming that spiritualism is a "literal fulfillment of the promise of Christ made on the eve of his earthly death," Johannes Greber mutilates the statement of our Lord. Here is his purported quotation: "I shall send you spirits of truth from the Father, and they will lead you into all the truth and be with you forever." Now turn to your Bible and see what Jesus really did say. Christ was not talking about "spirits" (plural) but about "the Holy Spirit" (singular), the Third Person of the Godhead. And He was not talking about the so-called spirits of our departed dead, but about the Holy Spirit, who is pledged to lead us into all truth. Jesus said: "It is expedient for you that I go away: for if I go not away, the Comforter [Advocate] will not come unto you; but if I depart, I will send Him unto you." "Howbeit when He, the Spirit of truth, is come, He will guide you into all truth." John 16:7, 13.

Take another example from the same writer. Here he claims to be quoting 1 Thessalonians 5:19-22. But see how he distorts the text, making Paul say things he never said. Here is Greber's version: "Do not make it impossible for God's spirits to communicate with you. Do not disdain the utterances of spirits through mediums, but test all that they say and adhere to that which proves to be good. Keep away from any kind of spirit-communication that has even the appearance of evil."

Now note what the apostle actually wrote: "Quench not the Spirit. Despise not prophesyings. Prove all things; hold fast that which is good. Abstain from all appearance of evil."

Misquotations of this kind are to be found in much of the literature of spiritualism. How can one have confidence in their doctrines when they so twist the Bible to back up their errors?

The Enemy Unmasked

When a nation is at war, it is vital to know the strategy of the enemy. And whether we recognize it or not, Christianity is actually at war with invisible powers, which Paul declares are "from the very headquarters of evil." Ephesians 6:12, Phillips. The church faces the greatest challenge of all time. But in the Scriptures the enemy is unmasked, and the issues made clear. We are engaged in no mimic battle, no mere dress parade. It is vital that we know the mind of God on these matters.

When He delivered Israel from Egyptian slavery, God told them to have nothing to do with the evil practices, including spirit worship, of the nations around them. No peoples of ancient times were more engrossed with occultism than the Egyptians and the

Canaanites at the time of the Exodus. It was God's purpose to separate His people from these debasing things. He commanded: "Regard not them that have familiar spirits, neither seek after wizards, to be defiled by them." Leviticus 19:31. Again: "The soul that turneth after such as have familiar spirits, and after wizards, to go a whoring after them, I will even set My face against that soul, and will cut him off from among his people." "A man also or woman that hath a familiar spirit, or that is a wizard, shall surely be put to death." Leviticus 20:6, 27.

In the light of these denunciations it is easier to understand the attitude of the early American colonists toward witches. We would not condone the Puritans for putting people to death on grounds of suspicion, but they were at least trying to preserve a pure faith. Spiritism in those days was anathema.

Note again the clarity of the Mosaic law in Deuteronomy 18:10-12. "There shall not be found among you anyone that maketh his son or his daughter to pass through the fire, or that useth divination, or an observer of times, or an enchanter, or a witch, or a charmer, or a consulter with familiar spirits, or a wizard, or a necromancer. For all that do these things are an abomination unto the Lord: and because of these abominations the Lord thy God doth drive them out from before thee."

Here is quite a list of the things being practiced by the surrounding nations. They were diviners, observers of times (astrologers), enchanters, witches, wizards, necromancers (clairvoyants), and consulters with familiar spirits (mediums). All are classed as abominations unto the Lord.

Other names appear in the biblical record, such as "soothsayers," "sorcerers" and "magicians." These, like those already mentioned, were prohibited. But in spite of divine warnings, "the children of Israel had sinned against the Lord their God, which had brought them up out of the land of Egypt, . . . and walked in the statutes of the heathen, and . . . did secretly those things that were not right." "And they caused their sons and their daughters to pass through the fire, and used divination and enchantments, and sold themselves to do evil." 2 Kings 17:7-9, 17.

It has ever been Satan's studied plan to destroy confidence in the Bible. In these last days we can expect the enemy of God and man to come, as the apostle says, as "an angel of light" (2 Corinthians 11:14) and "with all power and signs and lying wonders, and with all deceivableness of unrighteousness." 2 Thessalonians 2:9, 10. The Scripture says Satan is out to "make war with the saints, and to overcome them." Revelation 13:7. That expression "make war" is found sixteen times in the New Testament, nine times in the book of Revelation. These references are always in connection with the terrible conflict between light and darkness or sin and holiness. Note the warning of the apostle Paul:

"For our fight is not against human foes, but against cosmic powers, against the authorities and potentates of this dark world, against the superhuman forces of evil in the heavens. Therefore, take up God's armor; then you will be able to stand your ground when things are at their worst, to complete every task and still to stand." Ephesians 6:12, 13, The New English Bible. The Greek verb *stand* means to "hold your ground." It is not a command to march, to invade a foreign territory, for since the cross we live in God's hard-won territory. He has already won this territory for us. We do not fight *for* victory but *from* victory.

We can "stand" because, by God's grace, we have been "raised up together" with Christ and made "to sit together in heavenly places in Christ Jesus." Ephesians 2:5-7. When we have learned to *sit* with Christ in heavenly places, then we are enabled to *stand* before the adversary. "The Sword of the Spirit" is still the Word of God, and through that Word, we can overcome the adversary and be "more than conquerors." In the light of His completed victory we are to be found "giving thanks always for all things unto God in the name of our Lord Jesus Christ." Ephesians 5:20.

In that mighty name, which is both a title and authority, we present our petitions, for "that name is above every name." In that name there is power and authority. How many times we have seen the adversary slink away under the power of that name! We face a crafty, cruel, invisible, highly organized system of evil. But in the power of the Holy Spirit and by the authority of that name, Jesus Christ, we can be overcomers.

Seven times in our Lord's messages to the churches in Revelation, chapters 2 and 3, the promises are to the overcomers, the last of which says, "To him that overcometh will I grant to sit with Me on My throne even as I also overcame and am set down with My Father in His throne." Revelation 3:21. One of His last promises is: "He that overcometh shall inherit all things." Revelation 21:7.

Telling his own experiences, the theologian Watchman Nee recalls how he struggled for years to gain the victory. Then one day the Lord brought to his mind a text that opened up a whole new vista. In 2 Thessalonians 2:8 the Lord promises to slay the adversary "with the breath of His mouth." The Holy Spirit then impressed those words on his mind with wonderful assurance. "It will take only a breath from my Lord to finish him, yet here am I trying to raise up a hurricane! How foolish!" He stopped struggling and claimed victory in the name of His risen Lord.

Satan was overwhelmingly defeated at the cross, and he knows it and so does the whole universe. Let us thank God for the victory which is already ours and determine by His grace to be conquerors, yea even "more than conquerors through Him that loved us."

Paul's masterful statement in Romans 8:38 and 39 sums it all up: "For I am persuaded that neither death nor life, nor angels, nor principalities, nor powers, nor things present, nor things to come, nor height, nor depth, nor any other creature, shall be able to separate us from the love of God, which is in Christ Jesus our Lord." Hallelujah!

To be able to stand in the evil days just ahead will require a preparation greater than many realize. It is a war between truth and falsehood, and that war intensifies as we near the close of time. Events the like of which the world has not even dreamed of will challenge the stoutest hearts; and the deception will be stupendous, so overpowering, that it will sweep all nations; and Jesus said, "If it were possible, they shall deceive the very elect." Matthew 24:24.

In a later chapter we will see a movement taking shape that will embrace all the religions and philosophies of all nations. Only those who know the Word of God and have built their faith on its unalterable precepts will be able to withstand the coming universal delusion and endure unto the end. Are we ready?

Do the Dead Return?

"Ye shall not surely die." That was the first lie ever told in this world. It is also the basic belief of spiritualists, who declare unanimously: "There is no death." A spiritualist book, *The Truth About Our Dead*, declares that "death is as natural as birth. It is simply a transition to another plane."—Page 35. And again: "Death is another and more advanced phase of life."—Page 41. A casual glance at spiritualist publications is sufficient to convince one that "survival" is basic in their beliefs; that they claim there is no death.

From the beginning of human history the question of life and death has been of vital interest. Before death was ever known the serpent said to Eve in the Garden of Eden, "Hath God said, Ye shall not eat of every tree of the garden?" To which the woman replied, "Of the fruit of the tree which is in the midst of the garden, God hath said, Ye shall not eat of it, neither shall ye touch it, lest ye die." Then the serpent said to the woman, "*Ye shall not surely die*: for God doth know that in the day ye eat thereof, then your eyes shall be opened, and ye shall be as gods, knowing good and evil." Genesis 3:1-5.

Here was a flat contradiction of the clearest statement God could make. Acting as a medium for Satan, the serpent charged God with falsehood, declaring that if she would eat, not only would she not die, but she would be more alive than ever. In fact, she would live on a higher plane and would eventually become a "god" herself. This was the antithesis of the Creator's word, "In the day that thou eatest thereof thou shalt surely die."

Eve not only believed the serpent herself; she encouraged Adam to believe. By their act they allied themselves with the forces of rebellion. The enemy of truth had promised them much, but they soon discovered themselves criminals and paupers. Crushed under the weight of their guilt, and wincing under the lash of accusing conscience, they were driven from their garden home. The devil's lie had robbed them of their peace and their dominion.

Is Death a Friend?

In every age the enemy of God and man has perpetuated that same lie about death. And the tragedy is that so many believe it. Jesus called Satan a deceiver, the father of lies. John 8:44. When occultism tells us "there is no death," and that "what seems like death is only the beginning of a more wonderful life," remember that those words are but the echo of the falsehood uttered in Eden. That lie robbed the race of the glory of God, stole peace from the earth, and turned our world into a cemetery.

In the book *The Truth About Our Dead*, we read, "The declaration that each of us is a god in the making is as true as that a caterpillar is a butterfly in the making."—Page 69. And again, "All of us are gods in the making."—Page 2. Note the similarity of language to the serpent's words in the Genesis account. It seems clear that spiritualism stems from the same deceptive source as that which led man into sin originally.

Falsehood about death has cursed every civilization through the centuries. If death is really a friend, if we are better dead than alive, then why do we go to such lengths to preserve life? Why train doctors and nurses and build hospitals? If death is the entrance to a fuller life, then the sooner we die the better. But we know in our hearts that death is not our friend; it is our enemy. The Bible says: "The last enemy that shall be destroyed is death." 1 Corinthians 15:26.

Death came in the wake of disobedience. Eternity for the child of God does not begin at death, but when our Lord returns in power and great glory accompanied by all the holy angels. The apostle Paul says:

"Behold, I show you a mystery; We shall not all sleep, but we shall all be changed, in a moment, in the twinkling of an eye, at the last trump: for the trumpet shall sound, and the dead shall be raised incorruptible, and we shall be changed. For this corruptible must put on incorruption, and this mortal must put on *immortality*." 1 Corinthians 15:51-53.

Immortality is not something we possess naturally; it is something we must "put on." And we put it on at the second advent of our Lord. "Corruptible" bodies—those who have died—will be resurrected and put on "incorruption," and "mortal" bodies, those who are living at the time He appears, will "put on immortality." We are not immortal now, and we never will be unless we accept the Lord Jesus. "This is the record, that God hath given to us eternal life, and this life is in His Son. He that hath the Son hath life; and he that hath not the Son of God hath not life." 1 John 5:11, 12. Eternal life is vested in Christ; it is not something with which we are born. Jesus said: "Ye will not come to Me, that ye might have life." John 5:40.

Immortality, a Gift From God

When Christ returns, He will awaken His sleeping saints and bestow on them the gift of immortality, making it impossible for them ever to die again. Thus death will be "swallowed up in victory." 1 Corinthians 15:54. And this occurs "at the last trump: for the trumpet shall sound, and the dead shall be raised incorruptible." Verse 52. For sheer majesty and splendor nothing can compare with the prophetic pictures of our Lord's return.

Paul teaches: "For the Lord Himself shall descend from heaven with a shout, with the voice of the Archangel, and with the trump of God: and the dead in Christ shall rise first: then we which are alive and remain shall be caught up, . . . to meet the Lord in the air: and so shall we ever be with the Lord." 1 Thessalonians 4:16, 17.

This pageant of glory ushers in events which bring an end to sin on this old world. Then the righteous dead will spring to life again, and those that are alive and awaiting the return of Jesus will be changed, "in a moment, in the twinkling of an eye." 1 Corinthians 15:52.

The hope of the Christian is not death, but the coming of our

Lord in glory, which the apostle speaks of as the "blessed hope." Titus 2:13.

If one has the idea that those who have died are not really dead, but have passed into some higher form of life, then it is only natural for him to try to get in touch with them. This belief, we repeat, is the very basis of spiritualism. As expressed by one of their most authoritative writers: "It is as absurd to assert that the so-called dead do not sometimes return as it would be to declare that they were never born and have never passed on from this life."

The Scriptures teach the very opposite. Note these verses: "He that goeth down to the grave shall come up no more. He shall return no more to his house, neither shall his place know him anymore." Job 7:9, 10. And David, in his hour of grief, said: "But now he is dead, wherefore shall I fast? can I bring him back again? I shall go to him, *but he shall not return to me*." 2 Samuel 12:23. The dead do not return to us in this life. They are at rest until the day of resurrection.

The Bible and the Spirits

What about those spirits that appear in the séance? Who are they? Where do they come from? These are questions in the minds of millions,. Whoever they are, we can be certain *they are not our loved ones come back to visit us*. The Bible makes this clear and emphatic. We know that something does appear at times. Furthermore, such appearances have been known from earliest times, as we have noted. Ancient kings kept whole retinues of magicians, wizards, soothsayers, and astrologers, who acted as royal counselors. Concerning these counselors in Egypt, which was the very headquarters of spiritualism, the Lord said: "The spirit of Egypt shall fail in the midst thereof; and I will destroy the counsel thereof: and they shall seek to the idols, and to the charmers, and to them that have familiar spirits, and to the wizards." Isaiah 19:3.

God's original purpose was to use Israel to give the message of salvation to all the nations. Instead they followed the ways of their neighboring nations. Even their monarchs went the way of the pagan world. The attitude of King Manasseh is a sad example: "He did that which was evil in the sight of the Lord, after the abominations of the heathen." "And he . . . used enchantments, and dealt with familiar spirits and wizards: he wrought much wickedness in the sight of the Lord, to provoke Him to anger." 2 Kings 21:2, 6.

King Saul Seeks a Medium

Manasseh was following in the footsteps of Saul, Israel's first monarch, who turned from righteousness and sought the counsel of spirits. Of Saul we read: "So Saul died for his transgressions which he committed against the Lord, even against the word of the Lord, which he kept not, and also for asking counsel of one that had a familiar spirit, to inquire of it; and inquired not of the Lord: therefore He slew him." 1 Chronicles 10:13, 14.

Saul was an impressive personality. He stood head and shoulders above all in Israel. He once "prophesied among the prophets." 1 Samuel 10:11. But his lapse into spirit worship is a tragic story. On the last night of a misspent life he went in search of a witch. In defiance of his own command, and contrary to the express command of God, he attended a séance with a spirit medium, the witch of Endor.

This experience of King Saul is often cited by spiritualists and others as evidence of the survival and reappearance of "departed spirits." A few moments investigation should convince any reader that the whole thing was nothing but deception. Saul requested the witch, "Divine unto me by the familiar spirit." "Bring me up Samuel." 1 Samuel 28:8, 11.

The king had come to her in disguise, for he had given command to destroy all who practiced witchcraft. He "had put away those that had familiar spirits, and the wizards, out of the land." Verse 3. But when Saul promised that no harm would befall her, she proceeded with her incantations. The first information she received from the spirits was the identification of Saul. At this she cried out in terror: "Why hast thou deceived me? for thou art Saul." Verse 12. The devil can identify people, and did so with the renegade king through this sorceress.

The witch later said to Saul: "I saw gods ascending out of the earth." It is interesting to note that this apparition came up "out of the earth"; not from heaven or some spirit abode. Let us also ask ourselves, "Do so-called immortal souls dwell down in the earth?" Present-day spiritualism declares that our departed dead are far away from this earth; that they are enjoying a fuller life on one of the "seven astral planes."

When Saul asked the medium to describe what she saw, she replied, "An old man cometh up; and he is covered with a mantle." But *Saul actually saw nothing.* The narrative declares "Saul perceived" (that is, believed with the mind) that what this abandoned woman saw was Samuel. We do not doubt that she saw something, but it certainly was not Samuel. Is it likely that Samuel, the prophet of God and leader of the nation, the man who during life vigorously condemned witchcraft, would, even if such a thing were possible, come in answer to the demands of a witch during her incantations at night? Such a thing is unthinkable.

The whole episode was plainly the work of evil angels. It is evident that Saul received neither comfort nor assurance. The next day this poor deceived man took his own life. One can never contemplate that massive form bending over the upturned sword of suicide without realizing the awful price he paid for his willful disobedience. When he turned aside from the living God and sought the counsel of mediums he was fighting against God. The record of Saul's wasted life stands as a lesson to all who might be tempted to follow him into the sin of witchcraft. At the beginning he was the handsome king of his nation. At the end he was the plaything of the devil, dying by his own hand on the field of battle. Kipling has well said:

> The road to Endor is the oldest road
> And the craziest road of all;
> Straight it runs to the witch's abode
> As it did in the days of Saul.
> And nothing has changed of the sorrow in store
> For those that go down on the road to Endor.

Dare we go to the witches or wizards, clairvoyants or astrologers, for counsel? God's will is found not in the dark séance, but in His Word, which is a lamp unto our feet and a light unto our path. Psalm 119:105. Hear the clear counsel of the Lord: "When they tell you to consult mediums and ghosts that cheep and gibber in low murmurs, ask them if a nation should not rather consult its God. Say, 'Why consult the dead on behalf of the living? Consult the Message and the Counsel of God!' '' Isaiah 8:19, 20, Moffatt.

F. F. Morse makes an interesting admission when he asserts that modern spiritualism reproduces all the essential principles of the magic, witchcraft, and sorcery of the past; the same powers are involved; the same intelligence operting. (*Practical Occultism*, page 5.) In ancient times contact with ''familiar spirits'' was forbidden by God. Through Moses, God said that a man or a woman who was ''a charmer, or consulter'' was ''an abomination unto the Lord,'' and ''shall surely be put to death.'' Deuteronomy 18:12; Leviticus 20:27.

When the claim is made that ''spiritualism is God's message to mortals declaring there is no death; that all who have passed on still live; that there is hope in the life beyond for the most sinful'' (*National Association Year Book* 1961, page 13), is it not time to turn from the mutterings of occultism and seek the counsels of the living God?

Spiritualism claims that ''our spiritual progress is only the net result of our own efforts.''—*The History of Modern Spiritualism*, page 11. But the Bible declares plainly that we are saved by grace and grace alone. Spiritualism also claims ''we do not die.'' But the Bible says: ''The soul that sinneth, it shall die'' (Ezekiel 18:4), and again: ''The wages of sin is death''(Romans 6:23), ''all have sinned'' (Romans 3:23).

These claims are contradictory; both cannot be right. We must make our choice. Which shall we follow—the words of lying spirits or the infallible Word of God?

Bible Facts About Death

What happens when we die? Does the soul leave the body and fly off to another plane and live a fuller life? Or do we just die and that is the end? Some say death is a quiet sleep, an undisturbed rest until the day of resurrection. Others contend we are more alive than ever. One of the oldest questions in the world is found in Job 14:14: "If a man die, shall he live again?" How we long for a clear answer, especially when our eyes are filled with tears and our voice is choked with sobs.

Death Is Not the End

Deep in the heart of most human beings there is a conviction that death is not the end; that there is life beyond the tomb. Job did not wait for others to answer his question, for he knew the purpose of God concerning the dead. He said: "All the days of my appointed time will I wait, till my change come. Thou shalt call, and I will answer Thee: Thou wilt have a desire to the work of Thine hands." Verses 14, 15. Notice, he said that he would *wait* till his change came.

The Bible message brings hope for a dying world. The truth Christ proclaimed was confirmed by His resurrection. And resurrection is vastly different from continuous survival as taught by spiritualism and occult science. The Scriptures declare plainly that the life we now live is mortal; that we are all subject to death; that immortality is something God holds in trust for us. Not until Christ returns will we be changed from mortality to immortality.

The dictionary defines the word "immortality" as a quality or state of being exempt from death. The apostle Paul says we will "put on immortality" (1 Corinthians 15:54) when our Saviour

65

comes in glory. If immorality is something we must "put on" it is evident we do not possess it now. God alone possesses immortality in Himself. He is "the blessed and only Potentate, the King of kings, and Lord of lords; *who only hath immortality*, dwelling in the light which no man can approach unto; whom no man hath seen, nor can see: to whom be honor and power everlasting." 1 Timothy 6:15, 16. Immortality, then, is a divine quality. We do not have it innately.

No Immortal Souls

There is no such thing as an immortal soul. We will become immortal, but not until our Saviour's second advent. Then, and not until then, will those who have died in the hope of the resurrection be raised from their graves; from a state of corruption they will "put on incorruption." At the same time the righteous who are living on earth will "all be changed." 1 Corinthians 15:52. And that change will be drastic both physiologically and psychologically, for the natural body then will become a spiritual or immortal body, made like unto our Lord's resurrected and glorious body.

The apostle John says: "Beloved, now are we the sons of God, and it doth not yet appear what we shall be: but we know that, when He shall appear, *we shall be like Him.*" 1 John 3:2. Not until our Saviour returns will death be "swallowed up in victory." 1 Corinthians 15:54. "For He must reign, till He hath put all enemies under His feet. *The last* enemy that shall be destroyed is death." Verses 25, 26.

Spiritualists speak of death as a "friend"; the Bible calls death an "enemy." The difference is tremendous.

Death is an intruder. It came as the result of sin. It marred God's beautiful creation and turned this world into a lazar house. But when our Saviour returns to the earth for His people, He will bring an end to death. The prophet says: "God shall wipe away all tears from their eyes; and *there shall be no more death*, neither sorrow, nor crying, neither shall there be any more pain: for the former things are passed away." Revelation 21:4.

The message of the resurrection was central in the preaching of the apostles. The fact that Jesus rose from the dead gave birth to the Christian church. "With great power gave the apostles witness of the resurrection of the Lord Jesus: and great grace was upon them all." Acts 4:33. Those apostolic preachers of the first century—Peter, Paul, John the Revelator and the other disciples—fearlessly declared our Lord's resurrection. Because He died and rose again, "there shall be a resurrection of the dead, both of the just and unjust." Acts 24:15.

And that is exactly what Jesus taught: "The hour is coming, and now is, when the dead shall hear the voice of the Son of God: and they that hear shall live. For as the Father hath life in Himself; so hath He given to the Son to have life in Himself. . . . Marvel not at this: for the hour is coming, in the which all that are in the graves shall hear His voice, and shall come forth; they that have done good, unto the resurrection of life; and they that have done evil, unto the resurrection of damnation [condemnation]." John 5:25-29.

In the sixth chapter of the gospel of John we read: "This is the will of Him that sent Me, that everyone which seeth the Son, and believeth on Him, may have everlasting life: *and I will raise him up at the last day*." John 6:40.

Jesus was not talking about the soul's survival after death, but rather a bodily resurrection from the dead. It is because the dead do not survive that a resurrection is necessary. Moreover, the resurrection takes place when our Lord returns with all His holy angels, and not before.

Resurrection an Old Testament Truth

This truth is found not only in the New Testament; it is revealed just as definitely in the Old Testament. For example, Isaiah wrote: "Thy dead men shall live, together with my dead body shall they arise. *Awake* and sing, ye that dwell in dust: for . . . the earth shall cast out the dead." Isaiah 26:19. The psalmist cherished the same hope: "As for me, I will behold Thy face in righteousness: I shall be satisfied, when I *awake*, with Thy likeness." Psalm 17:15.

Those words, "when I awake," are significant. All through the Bible death is referred to as "sleep." We read that "David, after he had served his own generation by the will of God, fell on sleep [asleep], and was laid unto his fathers, and saw corruption." Acts 13:36. But like Isaiah, and God's people through all the ages, David was looking forward to the day of resurrection when he will "awake." In the intervening years those who have died are quietly resting in undisturbed slumber, awaiting the call of the Life-giver.

Lazarus Raised From the Grave

Christ demonstrated the nature of the resurrection when He raised His friend Lazarus from the tomb. When Jesus informed His disciples concerning the condition of Lazarus, He said simply, "Our friend Lazarus sleepeth; but I go, that I may awake him out of sleep." John 11:11. Thinking He meant that Lazarus was taking a rest in sleep, they were happy. Jesus then spoke plainly, saying "Lazarus is dead." Verse 14. The Scriptural figure of death is undisturbed "sleep." However, Jesus purposed to call Lazarus to life again. So He went to the place where Lazarus lay. And in obedience to His command, "Lazarus, come forth," that dead man awakened from his slumber and was reunited with his family. The Lord did not call him from another plane or far-off world, but from the sepulcher, the very place where they had laid him to rest.

In his recent book *Nurslings of Immortality*, Dr. Raynor Johnson ridicules this truth of the unconscious condition of man in death, labeling it one of those "foolish tales which has a long and dishonorable currency." He claims that the idea "that following death, the souls of men have a long sleep until some distant day of judgment when the worthy will undergo 'the resurrection of the just' presumably in their assembled bodies" has no place in the thinking of this generation. The sad fact is that Dr. Johnson has no place in his teachings for Bible truth or for faith in Christ, which he speaks of as "the childish imagination" to be put away with other "childish things."—Pages 239, 240.

And what does this spiritist philosopher offer in the place of the Bible truth? Nothing tangible or clear-cut; nothing on which one could base his faith. In place of creation he speaks of "divine imaginings," and in place of the Word of God he offers the rambling statements of mediums. And, like all occultists, he claims there is no death.

The renowned philosopher and magician, Apollonius of Tyana, who lived in the first century of the Christian era, but who probably never contacted Christianity, reflects the same old error concerning life and death. Writing to Valerino, who had lost his son by death, this ancient philosopher declared: "There is no death of anyone, but only in appearance, even as there is no birth of anyone, save only in seeming. The change from being to becoming seems to be birth, and the change from becoming to being seems to be death, but in reality no one is ever born, nor does one ever die."—Quoted by Douglas Hunt in *Exploring the Occult*, page 214.

These pagan sentiments of Apollonius contrast strangely with the clear revelation in God's Word. Similar sentiments are found in the *Bhagavat Gita* of India. Such concepts were challenged and overthrown by the preaching of the apostles.

A Description of Old Age and Death

Solomon's poetic description of the breakup of the human body is a literary masterpiece. He says: "The keepers of the house shall tremble, and the strong men shall bow themselves [trembling limbs mark the approach of old age], and the grinders cease because they are few [teeth decay], and those that look out of the windows be darkened [eysight dims], and the doors shall be shut in the streets [hearing fails], . . . and he shall rise up at the voice of the bird [sleep is broken; we become early risers], and all the daughters of music shall be brought low [the voice loses its charm]; . . . they shall be afraid of that which is high, and fears shall be in the way [the daring youth has fled], and the almond tree shall flourish [hair turns white like the almond blossom], and the grasshopper shall be a burden [insignificant things disturb], and desire shall fail [ambition is gone]." Why? "Because man goeth to his long home, and the mourners go about the streets [death comes at last]: . . . the pitcher be broken at the fountain, or the wheel broken at the cistern [no water can be drawn from that well of wisdom until the resurrection]." The silent form is borne away to its last resting place. But that is not all. "Then shall the dust return to the earth as it was: and the spirit shall return unto God who gave it." Ecclesiastes 12:3-7. The spirit, or breath of life (*ruach* in Hebrew), returns to its Source; the power by which the man has lived goes back to God who gave it. The power to live comes from God and at death goes back to God. "In Him we live, and move, and have our being." Acts 17:28.

What Is the Spirit?

Many seem confused about the spirit, not knowing how to define it. Why not let the Bible give the answer? James says: "The body without the spirit is dead." James 2:26. The Greek word for "spirit" is *pneuma*, the source of our English word "pneumatic." Those with marginal references in their Bibles will see that *pneuma* is referred to as "breath." This word *pneuma* is translated 288 times "spirit." But whichever word is used in translation *breath* or *spirit,* one thing is certain: *Without it, the body is dead.* The patriarch Job said, "All the while my breath is in me, and the spirit of God is in my nostrils." Job 27:3. The spirit that returns to God at death is not an immortal soul but the breath of life, the power by which we live.

When God created man, He "breathed into his nostrils the breath of life; and man became a living soul." Genesis 2:7. God did not breathe a soul into man; He "breathed into his nostrils the breath of life, and man *became* a living soul." When the power of God touched the inanimate dust, the lifeless form became alive—a living soul. It takes the breath, or Spirit of God, to make a living soul. So when the breath of life, the power by which we live, is withdrawn, death is the result.

This is emphasized in Psalm 104:29, 30: "Thou takest away their breath, they die, and return to their dust. Thou sendest forth Thy spirit, they are created." The Hebrew word for breath and spirit is *ruach*, and this is also translated "wind." In the Old Testament *ruach* appears 379 times, but not in a single instance does it suggest that man has a separate surviving soul, capable of conscious existence apart from the body.

Without the breath, or spirit of life, man has no consciousness; he is asleep. Paul wrote about believers who had "fallen asleep in Christ." 1 Corinthians 15:18. How comforting is the thought that those who have died are at rest. When our Lord descends the flaming skies as "King of kings and Lord of lords," He will command the spirit, or the breath of life, to unite with the inanimate dust, and bodies that have gone into corruption and apparent nothingness, will at the Creator's word come forth glorified. Having tossed aside their coverlet of dust, they will spring forth joyfully to life, "caught up together with them in the clouds, to meet the Lord in the air: and so shall we ever be with the Lord." 1 Thessalonians 4:17.

Bible Teaches Resurrection, Not Survival

Many outstanding theologians of our day, such as Professor Oscar Cullman of Basel, emphasize resurrection of the body as the true teaching of Scripture. If this were not so, what need would there be for the return of our Lord? For those who have always cherished the idea that their loved ones are in heaven with the Lord rather than at rest awaiting His call, this may come as somewhat of a shock. Yet a little thought will reveal the beauty of this Bible truth. Think for a moment how you would feel if loved ones had died whom you knew had not lived a life of holiness. What comfort could it be to you if you thought they had gone immediately to their reward? How much better to accept God's Word! Someday all will have their rewards. And in the meantime we can know assuredly that "whether therefore we live or die, we belong to the Lord." For "Christ died and came to life again, to establish His lordship over dead and living." Romans 14:8, 9, The New English Bible.

Death has no terrors for one who knows he belongs to the Lord. We are just as real to Him whether we are asleep in death or awake and living. The one who accepts Christ accepts eternal life in promise. The Scriptures make it clear he does not receive immortality at once, for *immortality is bestowed on us at the resurrection*. The interim condition of the Christian who dies is called "sleep." The teaching of a "never-dying soul" is unscriptural; it is vastly different from the beautiful biblical revelation of rest while awaiting the resurrection. One idea comes to us from Greek philosphy; the other from God's Word.

A large old grandfather clock stood in the lounge room of a popular hotel. It had been equipped with an electric motor and time mechanism. The sweet tones of its Westminster chimes endeared the old clock to all the guests. One evening a sudden electric storm broke over the city just as the clock was striking the hour of six. On the upward swing of the melody the power suddenly went off. For a short time the clock was silent. Then the lights came on again and the old clock resumed its music. It began its melody precisely where it had stopped.

So shall it be at the coming of our Lord. With the voice of the Archangel and the trump of God "He shall call to the heavens from above, and to the earth. . . . Gather My saints together unto Me; those that have made a covenant with Me by sacrifice" (Psalm 50:4, 5), and they will join in the music of heaven. Little wonder Paul called this the "blessed hope"!

The Truth About Life After Death

In the lovely rose garden of the Queen's Royal Castle in San-dringham, England, is a grave, simple yet impressive. A young prince had died at the tender age of fourteen. His father, King George V, although ruler of an empire that spanned the globe, was unable to save his suffering son. The combined skill of the greatest physicians proved of no avail, and the young lad died.

If you visit the grave, you will find these words on his modest tombstone: "In Thy kingdom he shall have peace." Amid the blooms of that lovely garden he rests awaiting the coming of royalty greater than his father. King George had to say good-bye to his treasured son. Even in that royal family it was true that

> There is no flock, however watched and tended,
>   But one dead lamb is there.
> There is no fireside howsoe'er defended,
>   But has one vacant chair.

But when the King of kings returns to receive from the world His own, He will establish His wonderful kingdom of glory; and in that kingdom all of earth's sufferers who have accepted His grace will find eternal peace.

How Real Is Death?

It was the serpent who said to Eve, "Ye shall not surely die: . . . ye shall be as gods." Genesis 3:4, 5. And that falsehood still masquerades as truth. Millions today have the idea that when the body dies and is buried the soul flits off somewhere to continue its own existence untrammeled by the limitations of the physical form.

When the pagans "changed the truth of God into a lie" (Romans 1:25), they corrupted the gospel. And in nothing is this more evident than on the confused teaching concerning death. Mrs. M. E. Cadwallader, editor of *The Progressive Thinker*, wrote her oft-quoted editorial more than a century ago entitled "There Is No Death—There Are No Dead." There she claimed that "belief in spirits is the foundation of all religions of the world." It may well be the foundation of the "religions of the world"; but the religion of Jesus Christ is founded, not upon belief in spirits, but upon belief in God's Word.

How clear the Scriptures are on this question: "The soul that sinneth, it shall die." Ezekiel 18:4. "His breath goeth forth, he returneth to his death; in that very day his thoughts perish." Psalm 146:4. "For the living know that they shall die: but the dead know not anything. . . . Neither have they anymore a portion forever in anything that is done under the sun." Ecclesiastes 9:5, 6. "His sons come to honor, and he knoweth it not; and they are brought low, but he perceiveth it not of them." Job 14:21.

These are Old Testament texts. But the New Testament is just as clear and emphatic. Speaking of the dead Jesus declared, "All that are in their graves shall hear His voice, and shall come forth." John 5:28, 29. Paul writes concerning those "which are fallen asleep in Christ." 1 Corinthians 15:18. He says, "As in Adam all die, even so in Christ shall all be made alive." Verse 22. And when does he say they shall be made alive? "Afterward they that are Christ's at His coming." Verse 23. These are but a few Bible texts; more could be given.

Spiritualism claims "that death is a change from the physical to the spiritual world; that the personality still persists in the world of the spirit; that those who have left the scene of their earthly labors can return to those still on earth."—M. E. Cadwallader, *Centennial Book*, page 86.

Both teachings cannot be right. Shall we believe the Holy Scriptures or the statements of men and mediums? Man's undisturbed sleep in death is a truth found all the way from Genesis to Revelation. It is emphasized by the prophets, the apostles, and our Lord Himself. Yet ancient Greek ideas still persist. On a tombstone in an old cemetery is this quaint epitaph:

> Under the sod beneath these trees
> Lies the body of Solomon Pees.
> Pees is not here but only his pod;
> He shelled out his soul and went up to God.

The Bible says nothing about a man shelling out his soul and going up to God. Let us hope that Pees died in the hope of the resurrection. If so, then he like all others who have died in Christ will come forth from the tomb, "at the resurrection of the just." Then, and not until then, will he go up to God.

Rest From Their Labors

The Scriptures say: "Blessed are the dead which die in the Lord," or, as The New English Bible expresses it, " 'Happy are the dead who die in the faith of Christ! Henceforth,' says the Spirit, 'they may rest from their labors.' "Revelation 14:13.

This beautiful Christian doctrine concerning man's quiet rest until the resurrection is given us for our comfort. The Scriptures say plainly: "The living know that they shall die: but the dead know not anything." "There is no work, nor device, nor knowledge, nor wisdom, in the grave, whither thou goest." Ecclesiastes 9:5, 10.

The word "soul" occurs in the Bible 488 times—428 in the Old Testament translated from the Hebrew word *nephesh*, twice from other words, and 58 times in the New Testament translated from the Greek word *psuchē*. In no place in the Bible is the soul said to be immortal, everlasting, deathless, imperishable, or never-dying. On the contrary the Lord says: "The soul that sinneth, it shall die." Ezekiel 18:4. Our hope is not in our possession of a never-dying soul but in our acceptance of the ever-living Christ. "For God so loved the world, that He gave His only-begotten Son, that whosoever believeth in Him should not perish, but have everlasting life." John 3:16.

One of the most inspiring passages in the Bible is this: "For the

Lord Himself shall descend from heaven with a shout, with the voice of the Archangel, and with the trump of God: and the dead in Christ shall rise first: then we which are alive and remain shall be caught up together with them in the clouds, to meet the Lord in the air: and so shall we ever be with the Lord." 1 Thessalonians 4:16,17.

Spiritualist Raynor Johnson classifies this statement of Paul's as one of the "tales for which corrupt forms of religion have been responsible." Declaring that "trumpets must have caught the imagination of St.Paul when he wrote," Johnson urges that we "look back and see in these 'tales' just the childish imagination of the race," then says, "in our maturity we put away childish things."—*Nurslings of Immorality*, pages 238-240.

Paul's word picture of Christ's return agrees perfectly with the other Bible writers. His was not imagination, but revelation. In Job 14:10-12 we read: "But man dieth, and wasteth away: yea, man giveth up the ghost [expires], and where is he? . . . So man lieth down, and riseth not: till the heavens be no more, they shall not awake, nor be raised out of their sleep." And when shall "the heavens be no more"? Peter gives the answer: "The day of the Lord will come as a thief in the night; in the which the heavens shall pass away with a great noise, and the elements shall melt with fervent heat." 2 Peter 3:10.

Attraction of Electromagnet

I was visiting a large steel factory a number of years ago, and high above me I saw a man sitting in a little cab. At the touch of the lever his cab went racing along over great girders high above my head. Then it stopped. At the touch of another lever a great magnet was let down over what appeared to be just a heap of rubbish. He touched a switch and then more than twenty tons of twisted steel, a shapeless mass, leaped up from that pile of rubbish. Clinging to the magnet, it was carried along to a giant crucible. When the power was released, the metal dropped into the crucible of molten steel. Later it was shaped into rails over which great freight trains race to their destinations, or made into cars or refrigerators.

The thing that impressed me was the power of attraction. It became a mighty sermon to me. I mused on what will happen when our Saviour returns. He comes with all the power of heaven and the universe. And when He calls those who are asleep in Christ, they will leap from their places of decay and corruption, millions of them, and "in a moment, in the twinkling of an eye" they will be changed into glorious, incorruptible beings. Not only those who have died, but also those living; those who are waiting and watching for His return, they, too, will be changed and caught up, and together join that mighty procession. Following their Lord, the whole redeemed family will go back to the Father's house and, sweeping in through the gates into the New Jerusalem, will be welcomed home.

Christ Brings His Rewards

When our Lord returns, He brings His rewards with Him. These rewards are given to the saints, *not at death*, but *at the second advent*. This glorious hope has always been an inspiration to God's people. Job said, "I know that my Redeemer liveth, and that He shall stand at the latter day upon the earth: and though after my skin worms destroy this body, yet in my flesh shall I see God." Job 19:25, 26.

The old patriarch knew that death was not the end, so he said, "All the days of my appointed time will I wait, till my change come." Job 14:14. In quiet sleep he waits; he knew the certainty of the resurrection. What matter if it be ten years, a hundred years, or a thousand? Time can mean nothing to one at rest. It will seem but an instant, because at his next moment of consciousness he will open his eyes to behold his descending Lord.

Do you recall the statement of Jesus to Martha who was sorrowing because of the death of Lazarus? He said, "Thy brother shall rise again." Martha replied: "I know that he shall rise again in the resurrection *at the last day*." John 11:23, 24. She knew the kind of life her brother Lazarus had lived, and she was sure he would rise from the grave when all the righteous are resurrected. But Jesus had come to call Lazarus back to this life again right then. Thus Lazarus would have a special resurrection. To resurrect a man who had been dead for four days would be a demonstration to the whole nation of Christ's deity. And the time had come for Him to declare Himself. Therefore He said to Martha: "I am the resurrection, and I am life. If a man has faith in Me, even though he die, he shall come to life; and no one who is alive and has faith shall ever die." Verses 25, 26, The New English Bible.

The one who dies in the faith of Jesus will come forth at the resurrection. And the one who has faith and is living at the time Christ returns will never die: he will be translated as were Enoch and Elijah. It was the Creator Himself who said: "All that are in their graves shall hear His voice, and shall come forth." John 5:28, 29. Why not believe Him? He is "the way, the truth, and the life." John 14:6.

There are many good Christians, and among them some of the loveliest people in the world, who sincerely believe that when a loved one dies he goes straight to heaven. To these we would say kindly that such a belief cannot be found in God's Word. Let us recall again the words of Jesus: "Marvel not at this: for the hour is coming, in the which all that are in the graves shall hear His voice, and shall come forth." John 5:28, 29. They are *in their graves* when they hear His voice. They are not in glory or on some other planet. They are right here on the earth when Jesus comes to awaken them. And like Lazarus they will come forth from their places of rest when Jesus comes again.

In the preceding chapter we quoted from Paul's letter to the Romans. But he wrote the same message to the Thessalonians. The Phillips translation reads: "He died for us, so that whether we are 'awake' or 'asleep' we share His life." 1 Thessalonians 5:10. We are just as precious to Him whether asleep in death or alive in service. We are still members of the family of God. How assuring is the thought that the loved and lost of other days will come forth from the grave to receive the gift of immortality.

> Although I grieve now you are gone,
> Black night precedes the fairest dawn.
>
> The flowers bloom, then fall asleep
> And buried lie in earth beds deep,
> Then rise anew when comes the spring
> To prove a resurrectioning.

Someday the Archangel's reveille
Will call you back again to me.

Then we shall share eternal spring
And view its glorious blossoming,
And all the stars shall shine anew
When love supreme comes smiling through.
                    —Helen Johnson

The Occult in High Places

As we set sail from Sydney, Australia, to New Zealand, some of the sailors seemed anxious. Seamen, as you know, are often superstitious. I heard one of them exclaim: "What! Six sky pilots on board! Matey, we're in for a rough trip this time. Maybe she'll sink before we get there."

He was wrong, for the Tasman Sea was like a millpond all the way.

Those "sky pilots" comprised four Protestant ministers, one Roman Catholic priest, and Sir Arthur Conan Doyle, famous as the author of Sherlock Holmes and one of the world's leading spiritualists. An impressive personality and a good conversationalist, he was on a world lecture tour in the interest of spiritualism, and he looked forward to a few days of relaxation on the boat. But he had miscalculated, for he was caught in a continual round of interviews and séances.

My cabin mate, a salesman for a large engineering company, was slated to spend two weeks in New Zealand. He lived in Sydney. Some time after we left Sydney, he said to me, "You know, I must be a bit psychic or something, because ever since I was a little fellow I have been seeing things. I think I'll have a word with Sir Arthur."

"You will probably end up becoming a spiritualist," I said.

"Oh, no," he replied. "I'll never be a spiritualist. You see, I'm not religiously inclined at all. I never go to church, and I never will."

But I knew whereof I spoke. He had the interview, and when he returned to the cabin he seemed to be walking on air.

"Say, friend," he said, "that old boy knows more about me

than I know about myself. As soon as I opened up the conversation and related one or two things he said, 'You are a premature child, aren't you?'

" 'Yes,' I said, 'a seven-months' baby.'

" 'Yes, and so was your mother,' he continued, 'and also your grandmother.' Then he gave me a lot of scientific data.

"I said, 'How did you know?'

"But he continued, 'If you know anything about your forebears, not only your grandmother, but your great-grandmothers for four generations have been premature children. You are the seventh generation and a male child. That makes you a natural medium.' Then he proceeded to give me all kinds of 'scientific evidence,' saying, 'If you will permit me, I would like to use you on this boat as my medium.' "

I asked my cabin mate if he was going to let this spiritualist leader use him.

"Indeed I am," he said. "In fact, I will have my first séance at four o'clock this afternoon." That was in just two hours.

Nothing I could say had any influence with him. We saw very little of each other for the rest of the trip because he was with Sr. Arthur almost continually.

Five days later, when we said good-bye, this man had arranged to accompany his new chief to London. Whether he did or not I cannot tell. But he was sending telegrams to his firm and also to his family, informing them of his decision. I have not seen him since. That voyage gave me opportunity to study spiritualism from another angle. I do not know all the "scientific data" Sir Arthur gave concerning mediums and premature births, but I do know that the stateroom the captain set aside for Sir Arthur was used for séances practically all the time, and there was nothing crude or clumsy about it. Many scores of the passengers took advantage of the opportunity, and among them were some prominent personalities.

Spiritualism Among International Leaders

Many ancient rulers consulted spiritists, astrologers, and magicians; and the practice persists today in high government circles. During World War II both Hitler and Mussolini surrounded themselves with clairvoyants and mediums. They attempted by these means to find out what the allied leaders planned, and especially to locate submarines. Douglas Hunt informs us that "one of Hitler's astrologers, Louis de Wohl, escaped to England during the war and was employed by our war office to tell them what advice their astrologers were likely to give him."

Another of Hitler's magicians was Erich Jan Hanussen, who was already famous in central Europe before Hitler rose to power. During the World War I, Hanussen (Steinschneider was his real name) was a private in the Austrian army. The army used him and others of his kind for consultations, for Kaiser Wilhelm II also appealed to occultists and astrologers for advice. Hanussen was a Moravian Jew by birth and became a close friend of Count Helldorf, the Berlin chief of police so well known for his brutality. It was through Helldorf that Hitler made contact with him.

Later Hanussen passed some remarks to Helldorf concerning the atrocities against the Jews. As a result, one Sunday his "friend" Helldorf invited him to a picnic. When Hanussen stepped out of his car, the chief of police shot him dead. It was reported that the Jew had "foreseen the end of the thousand-year Reich and unwisely told one or two of his friends." Note well: The mediums, clairvoyants, and astrologers in whom Hitler put his confidence could not show him how to win the war.

In a thousand ways Satan is seeking to win the favor of men, especially influential men. Some sobering articles in the Seattle *Post-Intelligencer* are examples of the modern approach. The articles are entitled, "The Psychic World—and You." The claim is made that the reader will be able to determine for himself just what "his psychic ability" is. But here is the writer's objective: "The purpose of this series is to pass along these techniques. . . . See for yourself. By employing them regularly, at the same hour every day, it is promised that we can tap the cosmic consciousness to become spiritual healers, dream interpreters, clairvoyants, mediums, through which *contact may be made with loved ones beyond the grave.*' (Italics supplied.)

The apostle Paul predicted these very conditions. Writing to a young preacher, he said: "God's Spirit specifically tells us that in later days there will be men who abandon the true faith and allow themselves to be spiritually seduced by teachings of the devil, teachings given by men who are lying hypocrites." 1 Timothy 4:1, 2, Phillips. The King James Version speaks of "seducing spirits, and doctrines of devils," and these will be particularly evident in the latter days. Spiritualism will play a tremendous role in world affairs just before our Lord's return in glory.

In the doctrines of spiritualism there is no place for the second advent of Christ, the end of the world, or the final judgment. Instead of Christ's coming to judge the world in righeousness as the Scriptures declare, spiritualism teaches that "man is the creature of progression, even to eternity, toward the Godhead"; that "each mind will judge itself." Moreover, "the judgment will be right, because it is the judgment of self. . . . The throne is within you," and "all men are unfallen demigods." Such teachings are a plain denial of the Word of God. In fact, spiritualism aims to "do away with theology" and "make the life of the spirit the all in all of religion."—*Centennial Book*, page 50.

Centuries before Christ, certain leaders among the Jews were saying, "Everyone that doeth evil is good in the sight of the Lord, and He delighteth in them; or, Where is the God of judgment?" Malachi 2:17. The same thoughts are being expressed today: "No matter how wicked you are, no matter whether you believe or disbelieve God and the Bible, do as you please; heaven is your home." To all such, God says, 'Woe unto them that call evil good, and good evil; that put darkness for light, and light for darkness." Isaiah 5:20. And again, "I will come near to you to judgment; and I will be a swift witness against the sorcerers." Malachi 3:5.

When men are led to look upon the Bible as mere fiction, a book suited to the infancy of the race, claiming it cannot be trusted and should be regarded as obsolete, the enemy of all righteousness is preparing the way for his final deception. If ever a people needed to be warned and counseled it is now, for a flood of deception beyond anything we have ever dreamed is about to sweep the world. And this will come in the name of religion when all religions will unite. Already so-called Christianity is extending the hand of fellowship to Eastern cults, and it will be but a short time before Eastern spiritualism will be fully united with western spiritualism. Then the whole world will be ready for Satan's masterpiece of deception. All unwittingly, both Protestants and Catholics, by their teachings of "survival after death" and the possibility of communion with those who have "departed this life" are making it easy for their congregations to accept the coming delusion. When Satan appears "as an angel of light," they will accept him as the Christ, not realizing that they are being dominated by demons.

Is There a Personal Devil?

Many today seem to find it hard to believe in a personal devil. Christ had no question on this. The devil was a real, personal being to Him, as to all the Bible writers. It is not necessary actually to see a thing to know it exists. We cannot see the wind, but its effects are seen, and at times it leaves disastrous results. So it is with the devil. The effects of his work are everywhere. To reject the idea of a personal devil, calling it a "childish concept," makes the chance of being deceived all the greater.

In time of war a stealthy attack is often more effective than a frontal assault, as has often been demonstrated in guerilla warfare. To blind one's eyes to the existence of evil is *not* to annihilate it. The Bible says, "The god of this world hath blinded the minds of them which believe not." 2 Corinthians 4:4. How true! A satirest put it this way:

> Men don't believe in the devil now
>   As their fathers used to do;
> They have forced the door of the broadest creed
>   To let his majesty through.

> There isn't a print of his cloven foot,
>   Or a fiery dart of his bow,
> To be found in the earth or air today,
> For the world has voted it so.

> Won't somebody step to the front forthwith
>   And make his bow and show
> How frauds and crimes of a single day
>   Spring up? We want to know.

The devil was fairly voted out,
  And of course the devil's gone;
But simple people would like to know
  Who carries his business on.
                                —Alfred J. Hough

Many titles for Satan are found in the New Testament—"god of this world," "the prince of the power of the air," "the wicked one," "the spirit that now worketh in the children of disobedience," "the ruler of darkness," or (Ephesians 2:2, Phillips) the "unseen ruler (who is still operating in those who do not respond to the truth of God)." The *New English Bible* reads, 'The spirit now at work among God's rebel subjects.''

Those who turn from the religion of Jesus Christ to seek the occult are turning away from truth and are indeed "rebel subjects." In these days we see phenomena of all kinds. The devil will even encourage a "revival" if through that means he can lead men away from the truth of God's Word and destroy souls. The most important thing one can do these days is to become familiar with God's Word and know His message for this hour.

The Coming World Religion

World religion! Can such a thing ever be brought about? Many today are saying, "If only the religious world would all unite, what a different world it would be!" And psychic power, in the hands of certain church leaders, is playing a large part in the creation of this new "international."

For example, "the Church's Fellowship for Psychical and Spiritual Studies" in England is prominent among the Anglicans. The official magazine of the group emphasizes clairvoyance, astro-projection, reincarnation, and séances, and all on the supposition of "survival after death." Twenty-five bishops of the Church of England are patrons of the society.

A corresponding organization, known as "Spiritual Frontiers Fellowship," operates in the United States. Its objectives are the same, and both groups operate under the auspices of orthodox Christianity.

Surely we are living in new and interesting times. The international climate is radically changing. It is significant when a pope solemnly begs forgiveness of those who have suffered through persecution inspired by leaders of the Roman Catholic Church in former ages, and at the same time assures others that they are forgiven for whatever they have done. That indeed marks a new day. Then in the same speech he urges Catholics to study the Holy Bible reflectively, and to be ready for open dialogue between Catholics and non-Catholics.

Where will all this lead? Can we solve political and ideological problems by a union of religions? Many believe we can and are working feverishly to bring it about. But mere idealism is not enough. There are deeper issues here than appear on the surface.

The study of prophecy convinces us that just before the return of our Lord the whole religious world will be united to a considerable extent. And in bringing this about spiritualism will play a major part. While it will claim to be the religion of Jesus Christ, it will really be the religion of the world, speaking the language of Christianity but guided by the spirit of Satan rather than by the Spirit of God. The Scriptures say that "spirits of devils, working miracles" will "go forth unto the kings of the earth and of the whole world, to gather them." Revelation 16:14. "Kings of the earth" could refer to more than earthly rulers. These will be kings of industry, finance, education, science, even religion. In Revelation 18:2 God calls this coming movement "Babylon the great."

Satan's Master Strategy

For years spiritualists and psychic scientists have been working for a synthesis of occultism and Christianity—not the historic Christianity of the Scriptures, but rather a new gospel of hope for mankind.

Forty years ago Doyle called for a reform in what he called "decadent Christianity," declaring it must be modified, simplified, purified, revolutionized, and reinforced by communications from the spirit world. This, he declared, would come about by "spirit communion and the clear knowledge of what lies beyond the exit door of death."—Sir Arthur Conan Doyle, *The Vital Message*, pages 12, 13.

He believed the movement would end "by being rather the proof and basis of all religions than a religion in itself and would effect the complete revolution of human thought."—*Ibid.*, page 31.

Harry Porter declares that spiritualism will "lift our civilization . . . into . . . the dawning of Christ-age" and will be "instrumental in . . . ushering in the millennium."—*The Miracle on the Wall*, page 286.

These are but a few statements from leading spiritualist writers, each of whom looks for the establishment of a world religion with spiritualism taking the lead. Shaw Desmond speaks of world spiritualism as "the white international" of the good spirits, declaring it will be a truly Christian movement "recognizing Jesus as its head."—*Psychic Pitfalls,* page 199.

Assuming a Christian guise, this coming world religion will prove to be the greatest deception of all time. The real head will not be Jesus Christ but Lucifer, the enemy of God and man. And he will appear as a great humanitarian and deliverer.

With civilization facing the threat of annihilation by atomic power, it is natural for men to hope for some great leader to arise—someone or some power that can solve the world's problems and bring about a permanent peace. He will have to be a superman, for only a superman can straighten out the tangled affairs of the nations.

The Scriptures declare plainly that such a leader will appear. He will come in the form of a man, but he will not be a man. He will be "clothed as an angel of light," and will appear on the international scene as a great leader—the most influential leader the world has ever known. He will be hailed by the nations of the world as the great deliverer.

Few things are as clearly revealed in Bible prophecy as the final events of human history, when the devil will stage a demonstration of deception beyond anything ever witnessed. Revelation 13 and 17 give a preview of this pageant when the world will unite against God. This union will be brought about under the influence of a mighty miracle-working power. Believing this power to be of God, people will reach out to grasp what seems to them to be the only sure way of averting war. In the name of Christ the nations will join hands, thinking to bring about permanent world peace. The whole thing will appear as a grand movement for the conversion of the world and the ushering in of the millennium.

In the vanguard of this movement will be spiritualism, not the spiritualism of earlier days with its crude rappings and mutterings, but something which so closely imitates nominal Christianity as to be welcomed by those churches to whom the Bible is of less importance than one's individual experience. Spiritualism already claims that the miracles wrought by our Lord Jesus Christ were performed by psychic powers. And it will be these powers that will unite all the religions of the world as well as the many different groups within the Christian church. But the leaders of this false movement will not be garbed in the cloak of ignorance and superstition. Rather, they will be robed in the white uniform of the laboratory researcher or the high vestments of the church.

How can a united movement of Christian and non-Christian religions ever come about? The following statements by Kenneth D. Constance, a prominent spiritualist leader, explain how this can happen. In *The Summit of Spiritual Understanding*, November, 1964, he says: "Spiritualism embraces every class of spirits, high and low, embodied and disembodied. There are lofty seraphic spirits. . . . There are malicious and greedy spirits. There are selfish and hateful ones." With this we agree. Then he links the movement with the ancient past, reminding us that Egypt developed communications with these spirits "as the very foundation of the national religion." Still reaching out to the non-Christian world, he says: "The great leaders of China, Lao Tse and Confucius, claimed to hold conversations with departed spirits. . . . Buddhism, Taoism, and Confucianism all embrace certain features of Spiritualism." Turning to the Greeks, he says that they had their shrines where "their priestesses were sensitive, spiritual mediums."

Constance climaxes his presentation by declaring that "Mohammed was a trance medium," and "Mohammedanism, founded in A.D. 567, was founded on spiritualism." While the Moslem world would possibly disagree with his claims, the one premise on which all religions could unite is the almost universal belief that the soul of man is immortal. Thus this spiritualist writer points up the possibility of a great world religion. When this finally comes into being, the great supernatural leader, Satan himself, will appear as the Saviour. He has long been preparing for this final deception when the whole world will be led to reject God. And it will reach its climax in the last remnants of time.

A Supernatural Leader to Arise

While in London, England, I read in a newspaper this startling announcement written by Edwin Lyndoe, a noted astrologer. He was speaking of the arrival of a great personality. This astrologer claimed he was able to make this forecast because of a conjunction of certain stars and planets:

"A great new leader who will deliver the world from chaos is about to arise. . . . He will be an orator with a bewitching voice. He will speak poetry naturally, and there will be music in his gestures. His knowledge will be colossal, and his judgments as nearly perfect as we can imagine. In everything he does there will be uncanny accuracy, and it is possible those who come into contact with him will feel they have never before met anyone so sweet of temper, so gracious, or so good to look upon. Wherever he goes people will love him and follow him.

"His chief work will be the breaking up of all the militarist ideas and institutions we know today. From the moment he begins his mission the armaments industry will use every ounce of energy, every penny at its disposal, to smash him. But he will win in a dramatic manner which will put an end to all those who have been building up the industry. His chief interests will be entirely public. That is to say, he will concern himself continuously with the alteration of social conditions, and for the first time in modern history democracy will have found its one superb leader. There will be no chance whatsoever for other interests to get a look in. This man will sweep the board with his opponents, and his work will succeed because he will be above nationality and above sect."

He certainly will be "above sect" for he will be of no sect at all. In fact, he will not even be a man. While the world will not know it, this "superman" will be the fallen angel, the great deceiver.

Bishop Fulton J. Sheen, of New York, one of the most influential writers and speakers in the Roman Catholic Church today, speaking of this coming superman, said:

"He will come disguised as a great humanitarian; he will talk peace and prosperity and plenty. . . . He will induce faith in astrology so as not to make the will, but the stars, responsible for sins; he will explain guilt away psychologically as repressed sex. And he will invoke religion to destroy religion. In the midst of all his seeming love for humanity . . . he will have one great secret which he will tell no one; he will not believe in God."

These comments, first from a leading astrologer, then from a Roman Catholic bishop, make even more impressive this paragraph from a prominent Protestant writer:

"As the crowning act in the great drama of deception, Satan

himself will personate Christ. The church has long professed to look to the Saviour's advent as the consummation of her hopes. Now the great deceiver will make it appear that Christ has come. In different parts of the earth, Satan will manifest himself among men as a majestic being of dazzling brightness, resembling the description of the Son of God given by John in the Revelation. Revelation 1:13-15. The glory that surrounds him is unsurpassed by anything that mortal eyes have yet beheld. The shout of triumph rings out upon the air: 'Christ has come! Christ has come!' The people prostrate themselves in adoration before him, while he lifts up his hands and pronounces a blessing upon them, as Christ blessed His disciples when He was upon the earth. His voice is soft and subdued, yet full of melody."—Ellen G. White, *The Great Controversy*, p. 624.

The astrologer said, "He will be an orator with a bewitching voice. He will speak poetry naturally. . . . His knowledge will be colossal." This Christian writer declares that he will be "a majestic being of dazzling brightness, resembling . . . the Son of God." And the statement continues:

"In gentle, compassionate tones he presents some of the same gracious, heavenly truths which the Saviour uttered; he heals the diseases of the people. . . . This is the strong, almost overmastering delusion."—*Ibid.*

This will indeed be a strong "delusion," but God's people will not be misled. They will know the Word of God, and like their Lord will be able to say "It is written." The same writer says:

"Fallen angels upon earth form confederations with evil men. In this age antichrist will appear as the true Christ, and then the law of God will be fully made void in the nations of our world. Rebellion against God's holy law will be fully ripe. But the true leader of all this rebellion is Satan, clothed as an angel of light. Men will be deceived and will exalt him to the place of God, and deify him."—*Evangelism*, pages 365, 366.

Importance of Knowing What Is Truth

It will take real courage to stand when all the world bows in homage to the false christ. The test will be short but severe. Prophecy indicates that at the very time the world is offering worship to the false christ the Lord Himself will appear "with power and great glory." Jesus said, "Then shall all the tribes of the earth mourn." Matthew 24:30. "And all kindreds of the earth shall wail because of Him." Revelation 1:7.

But of the righteous we read: "And it shall be said in that day, Lo, this is our God; we have *waited* for Him, and He will save us: this is the Lord, we have *waited* for Him, we will be glad and rejoice in His salvation." Isaiah 25:9. To resist the evidence of one's senses when all the world bows before the false christ, to *wait* for the Lord from heaven, will take real courage and faith. Only "the faith of Jesus" will make us victorious in that great and eventful day.

Our Lord said: "Watch ye therefore, and pray always, that ye may be accounted worthy to escape all these things that shall come to pass, and to stand before the Son of man." "For as a snare shall it come on all them that dwell on the face of the whole earth." Luke 21:36, 35. Phillips's translation gives this text thus: "You must be vigilant at all times, praying that you may be strong enough to come safely through all that is going to happen, and stand in the presence of the Son of Man." "Be on your guard—see to it that your minds are never clouded by dissipation or drunkenness or the worries of this life, or else that day may catch you like the springing of a trap—for it will come upon every inhabitant of the whole earth." Verses 36, 34, 35.

This deception will be short, but long enough to bring about this false unity and align the nations against God—long enough for every person in the world to declare on whose side he is—Christ's or Satan's. And the power that will bring about this anti-God union will be spiritualism. From Protestant and Catholic pulpits today, from lecture platforms of Eastern religions such as Yogi, Rosicrucianism, Buddhism, and Hinduism, there is heard the urge for unity. The twin errors of "survival after death" and "man's ability to become a god" are the basic tenets of spiritualism which will bring about this union of religion and politics. How important that every true Christian be prepared to stand in that great crisis. Some day soon the whole world will know the truth on this question, but for the vast majority it will be too late.

During World War II, a Scottish lady's husband was reported

"missing in action." She waited and prayed for his return, but it seemed certain he was dead. Well-meaning friends urged her to go to a séance and try to make contact with him.

She went, and to her amazement a striking likeness of her husband appeared. They chatted together, and his voice had the same lilt she had known. She felt a thrill as they talked about many personal things. But imagine her surprise and shock when a few months later her husband walked into the home unannounced, well and hearty. He had not even been wounded!

Someday soon, not just one puzzled woman, but the whole world—all who have put their trust in falsehood—will awaken to the fact that they have been deceived by the prince of evil. It will then be too late to accept God's grace. "Behold, now is the day of salvation." 2 Corinthians 6:2. If you are not already on God's side in this great controversy, then receive of His grace now. All you need to do is to say: "Lord, I accept Jesus Christ as my Saviour from sin. Give me strength to believe His Word and walk in His way." You cannot earn salvation, but you can receive it as a free gift. Then, whatever the future holds, you are a child of God.

A Final Letter to a Mother

My brother and I were conducting a large evangelistic program in the city of London, England, when our mother, to whom I wrote regularly every week, became seriously ill and was rushed to the hospital. I was not aware of this, but on the night I usually wrote to her I felt distinctly impressed to remind her of some of the wonderful promises of God, never dreaming that letter would be my last to her. In closing I said: "Mother, I do not know what the *immediate* future holds for us, but our *ultimate* future is certain. God may call one of us, or both of us, to rest a little while until our Saviour returns. But one thing is sure, we can pillow our heads on His wonderful promises" Then I quoted this passage from Isaiah: "Come, My people, enter thou into thy chambers, and shut thy doors about thee: hide thyself as it were for a little moment, until the indignation be overpast." Isaiah 26:20.

Continuing, I said something like this: "If it be God's will that one or both of us rest until the resurrection, it will be just as if we entered a house and shut the doors against a threatening storm.

Then when the danger is overpast, the doors will again be opened, and the very first face we shall see will be that of our blessed Redeemer coming in the clouds of heaven in power and great glory. Not only will we see Him; we will also see one another, and we will be 'caught up together, . . . to meet the Lord in the air: and so shall we ever be with the Lord." 1 Thessalonians 4:17.

In those days, before airmail, it took a month for a letter to go from London to Australia. When my letter, and also one from my brother, arrived, the rest of the family were at her bedside. As they read those letters, her eyes filled with tears, not tears of sorrow, but of joy. Taking those messages of love in her feeble hand, she placed them under her pillow saying: "Now I am ready to go to rest. I feel I have all the family with me."

With her last thoughts upon her Lord and her family she quietly slipped into her dreamless sleep. When she awakens at the call of the Life-giver, her first thoughts will still be on her Lord and her family. And what a day of rejoicing that will be!

To climax it all the Lord will make "new heavens and a new earth, wherein dwelleth righteousness." 2 Peter 3:13. The re-created earth will appear and will be the home of the saved throughout eternity. To His redeemed people the Lord will say, "Come, ye blessed of My Father, inherit the kingdom prepared for you from the foundation of the world." Matthew 25:34.

> Think of stepping on shore and finding it heaven!
> Of taking hold of a hand and finding it God's,
> Of breathing new air and finding it celestial,
> Of feeling invigorated and finding it immortality,
> Of passing from storm and tempest to eternal calm,
> Of waking up and finding it home!